How to Be Funny

Honest & Genuine Advice on How to Be Funny

(Releasing Your Inner Comedian and Improving Your Sense of Humor)

Kenneth Rosa

Published By **Phil Dawson**

Kenneth Rosa

All Rights Reserved

How to Be Funny: Honest & Genuine Advice on How to Be Funny (Releasing Your Inner Comedian and Improving Your Sense of Humor)

ISBN 978-1-7774561-1-5

No part of this guidebook shall be reproduced in any form without permission in writing from the publisher except in the case of brief quotations embodied in critical articles or reviews.

Legal & Disclaimer

The information contained in this book is not designed to replace or take the place of any form of medicine or professional medical advice. The information in this book has been provided for educational & entertainment purposes only.

The information contained in this book has been compiled from sources deemed reliable, and it is accurate to the best of the Author's knowledge; however, the Author cannot guarantee its accuracy and validity and cannot be held liable for any errors or omissions. Changes are periodically made to this book. You must consult your doctor or get professional medical advice before using any of the suggested remedies, techniques, or information in this book.

Upon using the information contained in this book, you agree to hold harmless the Author from and against any damages, costs, and expenses, including any legal fees potentially resulting from the application of any of the information provided by this guide. This disclaimer applies to any damages or injury caused by the use and application, whether directly or indirectly, of any advice or information presented, whether for breach of contract, tort, negligence, personal injury, criminal intent, or under any other cause of action.

You agree to accept all risks of using the information presented inside this book. You need to consult a professional medical practitioner in order to ensure you are both able and healthy enough to participate in this program.

Table Of Contents

Chapter 1: What Is The Best Way To Become A Humorous Individual? 1

Chapter 2: People's View Of Funny People? 19

Chapter 3: The Best And Most Appropriate Way To Have Fun 44

Chapter 4: Each Area Has Its Own Distinct Impression 70

Chapter 5: Humorous Types 84

Chapter 6: Maintains Relationships 102

Chapter 7: Laughter Decreases Stress .. 111

Chapter 8: The Benefits Of Humor At The Workplace 127

Chapter 9: How To Pleasantly Upset Your Audience 138

Chapter 10: Don't Be Afraid To Be Un-Funny 144

Chapter 11: Timing And Delivery 147

Chapter 12: Where To Get And Not To Get New Material 151

Chapter 13: Tap Into A Continuous Stream Laughter.. 154

Chapter 14: Man With The Humorous Reputation 159

Chapter 15: The Parallel And Opposite Story 161

Chapter 16: Tips To Avoid Politics Using Humor.. 173

Chapter 17: Greatly Exaggerate Your Numbers 181

Chapter 1: What Is The Best Way To Become A Humorous Individual?

Very few individuals are blessed with the ability to laugh. People can build it their own. It's not difficult to become a humorous person. Anyone can be funny provided he puts in the appropriate amount of energy into the task.

There are a variety of ways to become a comedian however, a few include:

1. Find a hilarious story to tell rather than directly smacking the joke.

Sometimes jokes seem like a framework. A typical punchline and buildup are present too.

Funny jokes can bring your attention to the plot. The form of the story has no impact on the comedy. It's there to provide support however, the funny circumstances involved will are enough to make you feel a little silly. This is how it is the humor that fools the brain. In the telling of jokes, there is an idea.

If the strategy is made clear, a joke can be deemed to be fake. The ability to have a real storyline flow throughout the course of a joke can be enjoyable.

2. The handling of questions using the opposite response

This is an easy method that can make anyone laugh. People already know what you will say whenever they ask questions. However, you could offer them a different response to the answer they are expecting. If you can do that you will make it enjoyable for the listeners. The concept seems too simple for it to work in real life. However, how brains function remains a mystery. Things that are unexpected can make people laugh. Brains are able to laugh because of something unanticipated occurs. Take a look at the footage from celebrity interviews in which this strategy is used. This is a straightforward method to engage the viewers.

3. Make a comedic quip from your personal experiences

An impromptu joke that is made based on an incident that has never happened to you may be shared. Some people may be hesitant to accept the joke at the conclusion. It is because of the fact that amazing comic brilliance can have an origin that is personal. Humor is always looking for a human matter. So, it is not right to repeat something funny and then claim that it was a part of you.

You should also write a personal note of your own. However, it shouldn't it should not be emotional simply since it's private. Discuss your personal experience. Others will surely be impressed by how relatable and personal your tale is. The unique stories you tell also provide unique material. The same trick has been employed twenty times previously. Offer them something fresh to laugh at with a joke that is new and original.

One of the best ways to alter the expectations of people is to use figures. When you're talking about how many people attended the event, make sure you point your guests away.

Make it clear that this wasn't an enormous event. In addition, you can mention that the fact that there were over 300 people in attendance. The numbers provide additional examples that they can relate to. It is certain that you will get a fresh perspective on the extent of excess and what is not enough. The secret to comedy is to move in a surprising direction. This is a sport that aims to outwit the mind.

Furthermore, they influence listeners' emotional responses. If you're hosting a huge gathering. You should acknowledge in modesty or conviction the fact that you had five guests there. Imagine attending a modest wedding or an intimate occasion. Make sure to mention that on page 85 of the guest book is the place you are. There are a variety of ways for convincing the brain to believe something while serving an alternative. Use the power of numbers for your advantage. Try out your own notions.

4. Do not linger. Get up to speed.

It is important to be punctual. Also, a long time could limit your ability to affect people. This is the reason stand-up comedians start their shows with five-minute routines. They must work to be concise. There's no way to tell that 5 minutes would be that lengthy. But, even a minute seems to be a long time even when you are in full control of your microphone.

It is the same in the realm of interpersonal communications. Avoid wasting time talking about boring facts to one another. The faster you are able to begin to get to the fun portion. Everyone is attracted by quick satisfaction.

The humor of the techniques allows us to experience that.

So, take note of the amount of time you're wasting while speaking. Make sure to keep your speech short if try to make yourself funny. The people you meet will certainly appreciate your sharp fashion.

Timing is a major factor in humour. This is why the rule of three could help. The pattern that is generated by this rule. The pattern then leads to an unanticipated conclusion.

Here are a few instances for you to think about:

I like honest, decent work, as well as cheese and potatoes.

The experience of being here is thrilling as well as thrilling and frightening all at the same time!

You'll feel cool, calm and generally a good person once we're finished.

It's a trend that's commonplace unique, distinct, and surprising. Furthermore, it's a great method to boost your mood. The creativity of your mind will increase when you come up with new ideas. The next time you're looking to show your wit, try to the challenge of trying this style.

Contrary to what many believe comics have more science-based backing. With these evidence-based arguments, we are able to look at comics in a different way. The truth is, having a laugh ultimately comes in the form of being genuine. Like we said earlier the sense of humor people have changes with time. People with particular advantages connected to their brain skills. Some, however, develop their humour in time. The reason why some people see humorous things interesting is an enigma. Each person ultimately decides their own direction.

So, don't worry excessively about proving yourself to the expectations of others. Concentrate on what makes you smile and see the humor within the process. The people around you will be there if you're content, as that you're happy. In those moments of laughter it is also possible to find communities. This is the primary idea behind comedy.

5. Bring a positive attitude about your

Smile when you hear someone say something funny to show your appreciation of their laughter.

Establish firm eye contact. If you are speaking with anyone, make sure you look at the person's gaze, but avoid gazing.

Keep a relaxed and comfortable body communication.

Offer a wide range of positive remarks and positive words. Look for the positive in the people you meet and your surroundings.

Be bold and don't hold back. Create ideas and share your ideas. Provide suggestions on activities and locations, such as. Let your ideas let others know about you.

Every person has characteristics that distinguish us from the rest of us. They may be exhibited in the moments when we're relaxed and are comfortable being the person we want to be.

Below are a few things to keep in mind when you're feeling uneasy

No one is monitoring your every step. Even though you might be, the rest of us are less concerned about themselves than you.

If you are unable to correct mistakes, you should think about the way a well-informed person would be able to react. It is likely that they will have no qualms what they did, so why should you?

Engage in conversation and show genuineness You will be more attractive to people. It is better to make a mistake than avoid speaking out for the fear of making a mistake.

6. Remove judgments

Other people will be relaxed with you if you don't judge their character. Be sure that you should give everybody a chance when you're prone to make snap judgements. Imagine each person as a possible friend. Find out more about your fellow colleague and be sure to maintain an open and unrestricted manner. Be aware that every person has something to teach you. Even if you'd taken a different path the choices of everyone else can be acceptable.

7. Take in the words of others

With your body language as well as the tone of your voice, you communicate that you love others and are willing to hear the people around you. It means that you put aside any other distractions and being attentive to the person that you are communicating with, while nodding your head, smiling, and sometimes making the "uh-huh." To demonstrate that you're focused, you must be certain to keep your eyes on the person you are talking with. Be sure to not look around at the space If someone is doing this, it could be assumed that you'd prefer to be somewhere or else.

8. You should be an extrovert.

If you share a tiny more about yourself by sharing a little bit about yourself, you can make it easy for other people to be the same. Be open and tell funny stories about your life and memories, like bizarre jobs you've had or a disastrous date or hilarious events that you experienced when you were a kid. Be careful not to share personal information for your viewers that may create a sense of discomfort. It is important to make your audience smile with funny stories. Keep in mind that two people need to be aware of certain aspects about the other to believe they are familiar with each other.

9. Do not be afraid to laugh at jokes

Individuals who accept occasionally committing a mistake generally are more pleasant to hang out with than people who are always serious. An error of a minor magnitude can allow other people connect to and appreciate you more. Pratfall is the term it's called. If you're able to be funny and laugh about it after you stumble and fall instead of pretending that nothing occurred, others will appreciate your personality more. People who are able to be funny about life and its absurd circumstances it places us in, are fun to spend time with.

Jokes about your life helps people connect to your personality. However, be cautious not to get too much into it. If you make numerous humorous remarks about yourself, other people might start feeling insecure.

10. Check out your strengths at.

Make sure to start by introducing comedy that will make people laugh, if you're looking to master the art of being amusing. Are you able to tell if it's dry? Words that are a bit silly and puns? Humorous body expressions and facial expressions? What ever it is, study the subject and attempt to replicate it with acquaintances and relatives. Later, you can incorporate the topic into your regular conversations.

The people who have fun are often a social glues that connect diverse groups, and aiding people in making new friends. Help your friends connect to one another by inviting them to meet the other.

Here are some tips to build camaraderie while having amusement with your friends:

Talk about common interests each of you has.

Ask one of the members in the class to discuss with the other members of the group something they've done.

Bring new friends together or friends to participate with activities that appeal to everyone. Examples include bowling themes parks, theme parks frisbee, soccer or game nights.

The brave people who are willing to try new things often come up with interesting stories to tell. If you tend to stay within your comfort space, you should push an extra bit. Take a risk regardless of whether they scare you. If you are asked to take part in something different, such as an evening cooking class, or even a speed dating session, and your first instinct is to decline but, be open to the idea. By gradually stepping outside of your comfort area increases confidence in yourself as well as your capacity to act spontaneously.

Being more optimistic will make both you and people around you happier to spend time with. As with eating more vegetables, or turning off your smartphone more frequently and choosing to remain optimistic is an option.

If something you're experiencing is causing anxiety think about whether there's an alternate perspective to consider. Keep a list of things you are grateful for in the event that something negative has taken up the entirety of your time. They are often things are taken for granted for example, being healthy and having a safe place to reside, being near to loved ones or relatives taking in nature or enjoying a good film.

As with other traits the ability to laugh is passed down through generations, however it is also developed by intentional efforts. A few strategies to develop an appreciation for humor are those listed below:

Read and listen to amusing jokes that are healthy for your health.

Watch funny television shows.

Check out funny YouTube videos, or any other internet videos.

Enjoy spending time with smart and fun people.

Develop your humor-making skills.

Develop an attention to detail and an aim to incorporate appropriate humor when it is possible.

Begin by introducing humor into your daily lives by sharing it in your home with your family. Then, introduce it to colleagues, your friends or even strangers.

In the midst of your most difficult situations, remember to keep smiling and keeping your spirit of humor.

The qualities one must possess or acquire to make one an entertaining individual:

Be Humble.

Making somebody or something appear bad isn't part of being a person with a ability to laugh. This is mainly about taking the time to be humble enough to admit the flaws in your character and the tendency to errors. This is why you are not likely to spend time thinking about your mistakes or blaming your self. It is easier to see the humorous aspect of a situation due to your humble nature since you don't place an excessive value on yourself.

Be Resilient.

There are always difficulties, however the capacity to keep smiling at the challenges indicates that one has an exemplary personality. While those who are constantly laughing can appear as uninformed, their comedy shows an incredible emotional ability. They are able to stay empathetic when faced with challenges

Be Smart.

The characteristics of a smart mind, like being articulate, witty and alert can be seen in humorous individuals. With their broad experience and knowledge their wit is often reflected in humorous humor and humorous jokes. The idea is confirmed by studies that show a connection between laughter as well as intellect (IQ). Thus among the initial actions to take if you would like to be the jokiest person around is to find ways that will improve your brain's capabilities.

Be Compassionate.

The company of funny people is amazing since laughter can be very infectious. Take a few minutes to spend time together, and you could be laughing loudly at silly incidents. Another reason to laugh is that funny individuals love making those who are around them smile. They try to erase frown lines off the faces of others in their unique method. The effort they put into this shows a caring and a loving mentality.

A life of constant stress is a bad recommendation because life is difficult and complex just as it may seem. It is best to encourage joy by making every day a cause for joy. If you also appreciate your humor, this will help you in a variety of ways.

Chapter 2: People's View Of Funny People?

In our society, we often refer to people who are hilarious to be "cool folks." It's nice to surround yourself with those who make people laugh and are happy do you not think? These people often exude an air of informality and chaos. What is the intelligence of these individuals? You might be shocked by the answer.

We'd like to inform you that humor is important in our lives prior to when we get to that IQ debate. Based on research the importance of comedy is various aspects, such as attracting people as well as establishing relationships. You desire career advancement.

Maybe you can find some clown or improv performances rather than enrolling in the costly course that you've thought about.

As not everybody has the capability of being funny as they'd wish to be. I have experienced it often and maybe you have it also. There's a laugh however, nobody gets a laugh. There are people who are going through hard time.

The jokes appear to require precise language, or in other words extraordinary linguistic abilities and the capacity to think imaginatively and come with different or contradicting viewpoints all at the same time.

Try telling an amusing story to you for an illustration. Imagine a monarch contacting an expert psychiatrist advice about how to conquer the whole world. The psychiatrist would reply, "Do what I say then you'll be king of everyone." It's amusing! since it hides the contradiction of contradictory intentions and actions. It's a key element in comedy, and when you consider the issue, it's more difficult as it appears.

The next time you are with an amusing person, attempt to take a look at them with a new viewpoint. It is possible that they are a intelligent person with exceptional ability to communicate, who is able to see the world from multiple angles and not necessarily the nerdy and snarky one. Be careful and smart!

One of the greatest ways to improve your well-being is to have a good laugh. Humor can be compared to your brain's defence mechanism. If you are exposed to a certain type of harmful stimuli, those that are susceptible to depression often experience depressive symptoms as they age, and then it is becoming more common for them to return. However, putting a positive twist on an unpleasant event can serve as a sort of psychological filter to prevent any negative feelings from sparking an emotional episode.

Humor is a shield against more than just depression. It also improves the general quality of life. As per research, those who have a knack for certain kinds of comedy have higher levels of self-esteem, positive affect confidence, self-efficacy, control of anxiety and the ability to interact with others. Yet, not every kind of humor is the same. The same study the researchers classified humor in four different categories: affiliation-based humor which is a type of humor that aims to encourage social interaction as well as self-enhancing humor. being a person who has a humorous view of life generally as well as aggressive humor, which is taking a joke on others as well as self-defeating humor that is, when a person participates in humorous jokes which make fun of themselves or self-deprecating.

People who scored high in self-improvement and affiliative humor have made positive contributions as mentioned above, however the self-defeating and aggressive humor associated with lower overall health as well as increased anxiety and depression. It is essential to choose an appropriate form of humor in making your way through the process of developing your comedy, as laughing at the other person isn't a great choice generally. general.Research shows that humor may boost your physical immunity, as well as being a part of your mental immune system. The laughter of laughing can also decrease the blood pressure, pulse rate and tension in muscles, that aids in the health of your cardiovascular system.

Along with improving your overall health, laughter can boost productivity. Contrary to groups that watched horror films or quantum physics classes people who watched comedy performed significantly better on an phrase association task that demanded the use of creative thinking.

The reason for this is it being the case that laughing stimulates the anterior cingulate cortex, which is a part of the brain that is connected to judgment and attention. In a different study, participants were challenged of creating captions that resembled the New Yorker the ones who took on this challenge came up with 20% more ideas over those who didn't.

To teach "the importance (and significance) of laughter to create an impact and create positive change throughout the world and - shocking! in order to meet business goals to create more efficient and dynamic organizations, create strong bonds, and make the most lasting memories" institutions such as Stanford offer classes in business on the role of humor in workplaces.

Everyone is naturally a fan of humor, however it's evident that not all people have the same sense of comedy. While studying theories of comedy is interesting and insightful but it doesn't guarantee that you will be more proficient in delivering an effective punch line. It's not pleasant to be told about all the positives of humor, and then discover that the origin of humor is entirely responsible for this.

The good news is that psychologists are divided regarding whether or not humor is something that comes naturally or something to be developed. There's nothing that can be said to make an uninvolved person since the ability to laugh is inherent in everyone. We were of the opinion that only certain people were funny, but the notion has been reformulated because of the fact that no social system was ever discovered which did not have humor.

Therefore, seeking out something funny in your life can be beneficial if you are looking to improve your ability to laugh. One of the worst things that could happen is that you may be a bit giddy.

People with more personality are found in comparison to others. It's a certain fact. However, is there any particular basis to this? Perhaps there could be a couple.

The findings of researchers have been found that supports an individual's sense of humor. This is the main reason comedians get hired for their humour. However, this doesn't mean that everyone has an innate sense of humor. Certain people possess the ability to entertain people. However, before we begin we must consider what is humorous. What is funny, and how?

It is well-known that humorous people usually are quick with phrases. Did you know that they also profit by this?

Jokes can help you become friends faster. People are more comfortable being around people with an attitude of fun.

It's therefore possible that humorous people pull others in with their humor. But, jokes and comedy are also a reason for people to feel vulnerable.

Punchlines can be risky to unleash. But, if the phrase is correctly delivered it could be worth it. The goal isn't always to make people laugh, however. In fact, making people think is the purpose. There are jokes that have a tragic beginning. In fact, many comedians make use of grim circumstances to create their comedy.

However, what makes them different from other people is their ability to put everything on the line. They are a bit sarcastic in their discussions about themselves. They can also bring some lightness to the room by adding amusement to the situation. There is more than just one character feature to be funny.

Laughter is a great instrument. Being able to make people smile is similar to being a superhero. However, you may not be particularly good at making people laugh. However, the tips below can help you to improve your comedy. Discover how to be funny through reading. It is possible to surpass the person with the highest popularity among your friends.

Take advantage of opportunities to sit with colleagues who are new, work within different sections of your office, or invite colleagues from different departments for take lunch. Although you may not be in control of the workplace you work in, implementing required changes may bring about a significant growth in the creativity of your employees.

The creativity of your mind will surely increase If you've ever participated in an "escape room" an actual adventure game that lets players complete the goals they set by solving riddles. Because challenges force players to use their imaginations and provide numerous solutions or suggestions.

In the case of a lock, for example, when you open a door and find that the door is locked, then you naturally think of options. The knob could be twitched or bang the door or even try to make it work with an Bobby pin.

According to Epstein the idea of challenging yourself similarly in your work, by setting an deadline or taking on the "ultimate task" within your industry.

Think about the biggest issues and issues in your field (How can I eliminate the world's hunger within one week?

It is not a given that people have more creative thoughts as they age however, they tend to keep fewer ideas. Make it a habit to record ideas when they pop up in your mind or just tiny portions of them.

Note it down on the form of a notepad on your smartphone, then write it down in a tiny notepad that you keep in your bag, or draw it on napkins. "capture the moment, then analyze it afterwards" since it has been proven that it's the most efficient method to boost your creativity.

Have you ever thought about the last time you learned something about medieval construction? An overview of the history of early Egypt? The wild herbs are edible? An interactive class or long-dive into the Internet might be the best option in this time. Based on research, knowing the subject you're unfamiliar with will help you develop different perspectives and radically new ideas.

"New concepts are born from the relationships between old concepts," and this can be demonstrated through an exercise that is known as "the experts' game." This is a group comprising of participants who present five-minute talks about a subject that is difficult. In the course of learning things such as the background of Rolex watches, or the process by which footwear is made, the group is then able to come up with at least three new ideas for products or products or.

If you don't take your smartphone to bed or in the bathroom, consider to implement this principle during your everyday activities. It's also an excellent option to turn off email notifications and notifications from social media apps. Set aside a certain duration of time daily to engage in creative thinking. Make sure you do this before you begin any form of brainstorming.

It is not necessary to deny that your problems aren't there or all of your circumstances are optimal, however. Positive emotions need to be acknowledged and dealt with. You may want to seek counseling if don't have alternative to your unhappy thoughts.

You can ask questions to other people to help them feel at ease, especially if you've got an inclination to speak only about your own personal issues. Also, you can search online for humorous questions to ask your friends for more information about their personalities. To ensure a balanced discussion, everybody is expected to talk approximately the same amount of time.

It is only possible to push yourself to a certain extent. In situations where you're in need of both mental and physical strength to go on recharge your batteries. If, for instance, you're at a gathering take a trip to the bathroom for 5 minutes. If you've endured a stressful week, allow yourself to relax on Sunday. The importance of socializing is over self-care since it's equally important to look after other people.

Everyone is unique. Be aware of the distinctive features that make you stand out from the rest of us. In the case of, say, you like death metal music and anthropology, you should be at ease talking to others regarding these subjects, when you think they share the same passions.

So long as you're respectful of the opinions of others, you are comfortable expressing yours. When you are speaking, take feedback from your peers. You should be open to other opinions, even if they're in complete contradiction with yours, and take the time to appreciate what is important in different people's views. Being open-minded is a wonderful trait. This means that you can have a great time with all people.

If we utilize our facial expressions to the maximum potential, they can have profound effect on people around us. Eyes, for instance, can become the point of exclamation during our conversations and can convey anger, shock and even confusion.

A. Thinking positively and the function in the development of a funny person

Positive energy and positive thinking is a significant factor with being a person who is funny. Funny people generally are positive thinkers. Positive thinking triggers thought that leads to a person feeling calm and relaxed. Stress-free people are more likely to laugh with others. If you're a cheerful individual, you'll be compelled to share your positive energy to others.

If you're an unmotivated person, you'll fill the surrounding space with toxic. The fact is that we aren't able to be positive thinkers by nature due to the current state of the world and its dynamic. There are, however, ways to get to a point where your positive outlook will be beneficial to your life.

Positive thoughts and a positive outlook can be the key to being positive about any issue. We could think that optimistic thinking is the state of mind that we are in. It is beneficial to think about positive results. The benefits of having positive outlooks are highlighted below.

If, for instance, you're a positive thinker, and you are a positive thinker, then you have an active, curious mind. The most funny people are usually always full of enthusiasm. If we are optimistic about our attitude towards life, we are more open to learning. In the absence of worrying about failure We also enjoy experimenting with different things. Similar to the children of this class, you'll be able to tackle difficult tasks more efficiently with a positive perspective.

If you are faced with negative thoughts that creep into your life and you are unable to overcome them by challenging your thoughts confidently. The research has proven that having a happier attitude improves your mental well-being and decreases anxiety. Furthermore, numerous research studies have proven that cultivating optimism is a helpful tool to combat depression.

People with positive attitudes are more productive over their peers as per research. They are positive and encourage themselves when they take on an exciting (or unsuccessful) task. increasing their chances of success as well as self-confidence. But, those who go to make unfavorable corrections and dwell on their mistakes have the chance of failing again.

The strategy is even able to transcend the boundaries of. It is also possible to consider the way it works within the workplace. Employers who are committed to happiness are likely to see improvement in productivity of employees. Humans naturally want being exposed to positive experiences as human beings.

Benefits from having a positive attitude can be observed in many aspects of work as well as daily life. Psychological, cognitive, emotional and social elements comprise the factors. The performance of employees has been proven to rise when there's a favorable work environment.

Employees are more productive when an organization creates an environment that is conducive to learning and has a good impression on the employees. There is evidence that shows both employees as well as coworkers gain from positive work environments.

Founders, social entrepreneurs and others who persist even in the face of adversity are recognized for their determination. This is due to a determined and optimistic mental attitude. If you are able to view difficult conditions from a more positive viewpoint, your odds to succeed are higher.

Naturally, having positive thinking is not going to help you go through anything. In order to reap the benefits of a positive mindset, we have to establish a plan to conquer that obstacle. The chances of achieving an positive outlook are significantly more likely if you blend these two.

We generally seek healthy connections both in our friendship and dating life. In this regard, we search for people who are able to establish healthy, satisfying friendships. A study conducted of a well-known psychologist shows how individuals can create healthy bonds.

The ability to be creative, humorous, relaxed and positive thinking are all utilized by optimistic people. All of these characteristics can help in solving disputes as well as removing the occurrences of negative attitude. If you adopt this attitude of positivity will generally become a more likable family member, friend family or a lover.

Treatments for recovery like physical therapy and psychological therapy take an enormous amount of effort and effort. Therapists are actually more inclined to increase their clients' ability to endure in order for clients recognize and maximize their capabilities.

One of the things that therapists evaluate in the patients they work with is their attitude towards the process of healing. The therapist will be conscious of this, regardless of whether you're trying to get back the control of your body or heal from traumas to your psychological health. A positive attitude will help with your development of your treatment.

B. What is the best way to use humor? How can it assist you in tackling difficulties?

Every person, in every scenario, could benefit from having a great ability to laugh. Each guffaw or giggle is beneficial for health and laughter can boost creativity as well as teamwork, along with analytical preciseness. However, at present the benefits of comedy are particularly significant in easing anxiety and tension which the coronavirus virus is causing to be felt in 50% of the US people.

There's been an undoubtedly an undoubtedly "huge stream of funny gags or memes, hilarious videos, and all sorts of snarkiness" due to becoming aware of the significance of laughter in stressful circumstances. However, while having a good laugh or laugh at someone's humor may provide an (welcome) distraction away from the stress of our lives however, to truly decrease stress levels and keep positively optimistic it is essential to make use of our comedy.

Everyone is affected by a dramatic rise in anxiety, stress, and burnout because of isolation from society, unpredictability and stress. But women are especially negatively affected.

One in ten males and one in four females have a severe anxiety disorder with physical and mental signs.

As compared to 12percent of men with similar circumstances however, 31% of females working full-time and having children believe they are overwhelmed with more than they can handle.

Stress or anxiety related to Covid-19 may have been a major contributor to negative effects on the mental wellbeing of 50 percent more women than men in this study.

In the study, 33% of females than males, the Covid-19 stress or anxiety has adversely the mental well-being of their loved ones in a way.

It is believed that "humor is the best inexpensive and safe method of reduction of anxiety, stress and tension, while simultaneously increasing an individual's physical as well as mental wellbeing in addition to promoting the perception of reality," it is especially amazing that there aren't suggestions to make use of humor in order to lessen anxiety and stress.

Under stress, those who have a spirit of humor "react to stress lower levels of depression, anxiety and less mood disorders" more so than people who cannot look at the humorous side of things. They also find amusement in the everyday.

Again, finding humorous in absurdity as well as alternative explanations for the complicated situations that we confront can help us find an optimistic conclusion. There is no need to just enjoy others' humor.

The horribly high death rate and the significant impact it has on those of color as well as the widespread economic hardship among the most prominent, are some of the numerous characteristics of the epidemic which are certainly not humorous. If humor is used to provide some psychological distance and distance, the most horrific events can be less disturbing and more bearable. If not, they'll be less terrifying and horrendous.

Comedy can give the illusion of having control over the situations we find ourselves facing. This is one of the reasons that "so many patients with cancer say, "If it had not been due to my sense of humor, I would never had survived my treatment and the illness!" They realize how humor can help ease stress.

Apart from the horrific consequences of the pandemic, a lot of the circumstances which we're in are bizarre, such as having to spend every day at the same place either by ourselves or in the company of similar persons, navigating through glitches and issues with video conferencing to mention the few. It is easier to face our present situation with a laugh or a smile, even if that smile is just sarcastic or ironic when we know the absurdity and bizarre nature of some of the elements are.

Everybody, and women specifically, are able to keep a positive outlook during these times of stress through looking for humor in their circumstances their own lives, as well as in their own absurdity. are.

There are a variety of strategies that you could try out if think your sense of laughter is lacking:

Pick one or two strange or bizarre things to be aware of every daily. Imagine these things multiplied by 10 10, 20, or even 100, to an absurd level You will discover amusing and worthy of laughter.

Tell short, humorous stories of your frustrations and insecurities to colleagues as well as your friends,. You're trying to become someone who is able to transform bitter into semi-sweet. You are not an actor.

Listen, read or see monologues, stories, tweets, GIFs, and short amusing or funny films. Make changes or expand the ones which are particularly relevant to your needs as you come across the best ones to convey the humor in the situation. The revised vignettes must be shared with your family, colleagues and friends.

Remember that what you think is funny might not appeal to others. Think about your favorite things that make you laugh or smile. Then look for the same things within your surroundings.

Chapter 3: The Best And Most Appropriate Way To Have Fun

My very first tip for cultivating a sense humor is also one of the most challenging. It is essential to master the art of surprise to improve your comedy.

Each joke or funny story centers around the concept of surprise. The only method to bring anyone to smile is to make them laugh. As it takes away the possibility of surprise jokes lose its charm if its joke's punchline is already known. Videos like this are found extremely entertaining due to these motives:

Puns, even though they are some of the simplest jokes require a bit of some kind of. In the instance of the time my father shared the tale of his sweater I thought I was hearing an ordinary routine story. However suddenly I was shocked by the punch line (albeit an extremely inadequate one) which he uttered.

Take a look at some funny jokes that you think are hilarious. Find any signs that are surprising in them. What do the viewers anticipate? And how will the surprise of the story make them awestruck?

Looking at jokes such as this can be an excellent starting point, however these tips will allow you to make people laughter before they are expecting it.

To master the art of unexpectedness and develop the ability to laugh you must be aware:

You must be aware of the world around you in order to find the surprising joke that no one else is aware of. The goal is to find unusual, odd funny, humorous, and sardonic things in the world around you.

The ability to observe in a range different methods. A regular practice of meditation and reflection and writing down your thoughts, making photos or videos, or having deep conversations with your acquaintances are great ways to get started.

No matter what method you pick take, be on the lookout for funny moments, even during your day-to-day routine.

The best way to test it is to check it at your local second-hand store before you go to the secondhand shop. You can spend ten minutes in there and I'm sure you'll come across a strange T-shirt or other object that will make your smile. If you find something, stop to think about what is it in the context that causes you smile. What is the reason for it?

As you continue to practice this sort of deliberate observation, the better you'll learn to notice funny situations as they occur.

The most rewarding homework assignment I've ever offered you is set to begin.

It is important to observe hilarious individuals if you wish to know how to come off as funny.

There's plenty of opportunities for you to watch seasoned comedians performing their craft today, due to Netflix as well as YouTube.

In addition, there is a wealth of comical podcasts and books that can be discovered.

It's time to expand your horizons once you've learned about the comedian you love in-depth. You can watch the latest Netflix series that stars a newcomer that doesn't look like any of your favorites in looks or manner of speaking. Participate in a comedy performance in your area, in which you don't know exactly what you can expect. Find three comedy podcasts to add to your subscription list.

Think of humor as something you can sample before returning for additional of your favorite. Soon, you'll become your own unique comedy voice.

Additional advice: Take notes whenever you encounter a comedian that you don't find amusing. What's the issue with the manner in which they perform, how they speak or the topic they are not happy with? It is equally important to consider, particularly with regard to my next suggestion.

An impromptu joke that you can make on a first date is likely to be distinct from the one you tell your best pal. Your grocery store employee could simply look at you with an uninterested look after you tell a joke which makes mom laugh.

How can you improve your the ability to read in a room?

It is all about the capacity to observe. It is important to be mindful of those you share a space along with being attentive to the surroundings. It is important to consider the identity of those you are with and their circumstances at that time as well as their knowledge about you. The room is read using the entire information.

An effective joke requires an artist's skill to come up with. It's a lot more challenging to figure out how to create a laughable joke repeatedly and yet, if you can this, it's one of the best things to ever happen.

There are a variety of comedians that perform this. The joke is usually told during the opening of a show, and at the point that audiences least anticipate it, the exact joke is repeated (with an added twist).

If you are looking for private moments of fun between your friends or spouses, jokes about running are a great option. These jokes can be a form of joke inside that one person and you could employ repeatedly in order in order to have fun with each other.

You need to be aware of the things that make people laugh in order to make successful running jokes. Also, it is important to strike an equilibrium between creating an entertaining running gag as well as stumbling over jokes from the past. You know it's time to end the joke when people begin to smile more and laugh less after having repeatedly told the joke.

A different saying that you've probably encountered before is instead of making fun of yourself, you'd like for people to be with your laughter.

The key to self-deprecating comedy According to the experts, it is every time you're the joke's end phrase.

If the comedy comes through a trusted source, it could be very effective. There is a difference between laughing yourself silly in the spirit of forgiveness and compassion or because of a genuine hatred of your self is huge. (If you attempt to get people laughing you will fail.)

When you make use of self-deprecating humor you're saying to the audience "I am very aware of myself, therefore I'm able to enjoy myself without harming anyone else. You are also invited to join me in this."

We'll discuss the things that aren't humorous in my final bit of tips. Since knowing when to laugh and also when you should hold your mouth is a crucial capability if you're hoping to be perceived as an entertainer.

The circumstances you're facing must be considered at the beginning. The idea of laughing while drinking the company of friends is fine; however, making snarky remarks in a funeral service isn't.

A comedian who is good at his job can determine the boundaries between what's or is not funny, because they're in the know of where that line is. But, they will be in a depressing region once you reach the threshold.

Be sure to keep your jokes "free of harm" If you wish not to go overboard. It is not funny if they actually harm someone else, regardless of whether you're making fun of you or an ordinary situation.Nothing can be more entertaining than viewing footage of bizarre animals. Watching videos of infants doing silly things can be enjoyable. To find hilarious videos on YouTube you can just click whenever you're feeling low and want to have a laughter. There is bound to be things that make you smile.

You can also opt to be a follower of YouTubers who get paid to make others smile. You will then get a steady stream of hilarious videos to watch.

The sharing of stories about hilarious moments is the most enjoyable thing you can do. No matter if you're using FaceTime, Zoom, or Skype you can think about the time you spent together and enjoy a great time with the absurd incidents you've committed. You can share an "Remember that time when" story in the next time you talk to an acquaintance or member of your family. You will surely bring both of you smiles.

Have fun playing a game of board with your friends in the event that you're staying in your home. While playing games with complicated questions, it does not take long to make everyone let go of the troubles that are part of everyday routine. Playing strategy games such as Monopoly and Sequence will make your house much more enjoyable and fun.

If you are feeling lonely and lonely, think about throwing an online gaming event. As an example, Jackbox Games provides a large selection of digital gaming platforms for customers to buy and download games for playing online. Additionally, they are able to create game-themed parties with at least eight players.

There are a lot of actions that you do that, if taken an extra step back and looked at them, you'd discover to be hilarious. Maybe it's because the hair that's swept to your sides sticks away from your mask. Perhaps it's because you went to your partner's Zoom meeting in your shorts. You could have unintentionally included that huge Captain America cutout in a professional-looking video that you had been filming and didn't realize you did it.

Everybody makes a mistake. It is important to periodically laugh at yourself. The moment you laugh you inspire others to laugh too.

A popular and popular and widely utilized social media apps is TikTok. It is used by people to come up with their own hilarious versions of everything from being at home and avoiding the issue of toilet paper in this outbreak, and they're taking part in large quantities.

Online creators are able to raise money for relief efforts from coronavirus through TikTok's donation sticker. Medical professionals as well as experts in the business are making use of this app to relay important details to children. The app can be downloaded, and later when you are looking for to have a good laugh, and you've got an extra few minutes.

1. Open yourself up

It is important to prepare yourself for that the potential audience may not be able to grasp your message. Keep in mind that not all attempts you attempt to make amusing can be completely successful. The key is being committed. Comedy is nothing like this.

Professional comedians' jokes often fail to be funny. However, they do get better at moving on to their next gag.

2. Utilize your own personal experiences as a source of inspiration

It's not unless you see the humorous in getting locked out of your hotel room, with just an untied waistband. An effective way to inject the humor in your life is to allow your friends and family make fun of your shortcomings (maybe using a few humorous anecdotes). Also, it has been proven that humorous real life stories are more likely to get people laughing more.

3. Watch comedic shows on television or via the internet.

We know that watching experts help us when we are looking to become more proficient at a particular thing. It's the same for becoming more humorous. Make popcorn and put on a show that is funny. When "studying" the shows ask yourself these questions How did I come to enjoy this segment? What was the thing that the actor said or do during this particular scene that got me laughing?

In addition, you can witness how the audience reacts to an individual joke. Note down what you enjoy that the comedians differ from one another. Your comedy sense will benefit by the data you have gathered.

4. Learn about the context

Humor requires context in order to be effective. Based on a study, funny situations have an "rise and rise and." The study found that there's a waiting time for when something bad happens to be amusing. They also found that at this point the show is no longer funny.

If you are planning to play humorous remarks about the current situation be aware of this.

5. Take a look at comedy movies and enjoy the comedy

Watching amusing films is an excellent way to uncover your inner comedy. Comedy films are the ideal place to begin.

Take note of your most loved aspects in films. It is possible to look at other films that have the same theme. For the best enjoyment from this exercise, be sure to watch films with the fullest of detail.

6. You have a joke that you are able to deliver confidently

At a minimum, you should have one joke that is universally applicable in your arsenal. Find out how to tell your story in a manner which will get people laughing.

7. Note what you consider funny.

Pay at what others enjoy if you are looking to improve your communication skills. Certain people think they are able to predict what makes people laugh, yet cause them to be offended. Avoid this kind of man.

8. Your true self is you

When you've got your ability to laugh You should be careful not to make jokes on other people. Furthermore, it doesn't require you to act extravagantly or foolishly.

Simply stated, the ability to effectively draw out the funny in an environment could be sufficient to be an interesting and charming individual.

9. Establish an objective view

A majority of people evaluate a situation following a close glance. This can lead to negative thinking.

There is no way to have fun when you're being judgmental. Your opinion will always be out of line with your ability to see the bigger picture, more fun of a specific situation. Do not take this route. This blog will help you understand the ways to not be so pessimistic.

10. Do some linguistic improvement

Many people laugh when someone is funny and is quick to make a comment. They typically use the language in a way other people do not.

Improve your language skills. Learn to improve your grammar and the vocabulary you have. If you're in need of help Begin by contemplating what you can say regarding these hilariously contentious topics.

11. Believe in your funny talents

Finding your humor isn't easy and can cause a lot of stress. You have do your act before people. The growth mindset can assist with the process of improving your skill. In order to be successful in making others smile, do as much as you can, and then master every aspect you can.

12. Find the funny everywhere

It's acceptable to show your displeasure at unfortunate incidents such as accidentally throwing one of your red socks in the wash along with your whites, or walking through dog's poop in new shoes. The result is nothing other than making you unhappy for the rest of your day. Consider that this same scenario occurs to someone else. Make fun of that person. Then, you'll be able to laugh with yourself too.

The ability to laugh can improve by focusing on the absurdity in a sad stressful, irritating or tension-filled scenario. Be sure that you should keep your jokes in line with the current.

13. Meet a funny partner

Your accountability buddy is in the form of your hilarious friend. The person you trust can aid you with enhancing your recently gained skills.

You practice regularly your jokes with the person and employ him or her as the yardstick for determining the truth of what you're saying is humorous. This helps you stay committed to the goal, by making accountable.

14. Laugh

Being able to make other people laugh isn't the only reason to have the ability to laugh. Also, it can bring lots of laughs.

One thing you should remember is that you shouldn't make up a show of grace and air or act like somebody you're not the hopes of being funny. The influence of some of the most famous comedians in the world is great however, making your own unique style of comedy is different. It is true that most comedians around the world possess distinct style. They're popular and successful with their craft because of that. The same objectives for your own self. It is essential to be honest in order to be successful.

The most popular jokes people like are those they are able to relate to. You should try to make jokes around topics that relate to your personal life, human nature in the present, as well as the everyday life you lead. Naturally, knowing and understanding the audience is a key element in the process. Finding jokes that are relatable to the people you love are significantly easier than performing the same for an entire group of audience members at a show. It is important to know the audience's needs and the things that matter to their needs.

A few of your common jokes, or one-liners can be used over and over again should not shame yourself about. You may have made some jokes before and had the audience laughing. Perhaps you've got a handful of catchy quotes and phrases that will always get people laughing. Find a handful of your most memorable gags and then use to begin a conversation. In the event of meeting someone new, and it doesn't appear to be progressing This can be extremely useful. Make it short and concise The message does not have to be lengthy or sloppy.

Another horrible word you're learning. It's not an exam So, don't worry! But when you are trying to learn new skills it is our belief that there are many benefits when you read the book. Like any other skill the ability to be funny can be learned.

The theories that underlie humor are the focus of countless blogs, books, as well as journal article. The process of reading about these ideas prior to taking them on the field is the best way to acquire knowledge.

"The one of our top "funny" strategies is this method. It works every time. This is achieved by being vague and a little bit sarcastic. It is most effective in conversations with someone because you are able to effortlessly drop a joke and then wait for inevitable laughter. Saying something that is not to be expected from you will do the trick.

As an example, when somebody asks "Did you make it to the station in time?" The answer could be "No...the train ran late because an enormous donut landed on the tracks," or something similar. If someone else wants to know if you're okay and you are not, just reply "No" prior to going on to clarify that you're in fact "half still."

Everyone has one distinctive voice that can be a vital tool in being funny. The same thing isn't requiring any effort because it is a natural trait for us. The ability to make something appear to be more hilarious than it really is simply by changing your tone of voice.

Tone of voice is responsible for 38% of the effectiveness of communication. Getting this correct can transform your comedy from boring to dazzling! You can experiment using your voice's tone using words that are supposed to be a joy to you are serious or depressing.

This may seem to be completely absurd, but bear in with us as we describe. Imagine interacting with someone in the manner that follows. This is the complete guide to being humorous. You already know that you've got the skills to be funny. Although we may not have the desire to you can easily achieve It.

Actually, certain that your buddies consider you to be the most fun person they've met.

However, since making others smile is among the most enjoyable feelings anywhere it is easy to understand the desire to become even more hilarious.

Although you may have a distinct brand of humor There are many helpful tips within this "how to become funny" that you'll enjoy using. It is always wise to be aware that every person in the world differs from each other with different preferences and dislikings. It's a fact that regardless of your best efforts, there will always some people who think that you are not funny.

However, what do you think? It's fine since you already know people who don't seem to be hilarious. Don't worry about it. Just save your jokes for people who find them entertaining and then share a bit of what you've learned to them too.

What is it that are part of that category "not to be done" for the purpose of becoming comedians?

1. Avoid being blitzed. How can you treat live theatre with such a sour attitude in the event that you wouldn't be exhausted halfway through Les Miserables? The majority of comedy venues have the two drink minimum. this isn't easy. If you are able to do it. Alcohol helps keep our wage being paid. If not, keep a water bottle for your next drink.

2. Be wary of answering rhetorical questions. Do you understand what I'm trying to say?

3. Make quiet orders. If possible, point silently towards what you would like. It is important to be conscious that the cocktail servers belong to those that are most skilled in interpreting the meaning of gestures.

4. Don't talk for too long. Do not provide a long explanation if a comedian asks you a question. It is not like you are dating them in the very first time. They're simply making use of the situation as an opportunity to divert attention.

5. Beware of texting. Are you ever using your phone to light up at night? This is because it illuminates the dimness of a room. Science!

6. Be careful not to dress in a manner that draws a lot of people's attention. There are people who dress like jerks, comics who snarkily pick at people. However there was a guy in front of me that was dressed in an armor suit constructed from beer cans. It was awe-inspiring, yet annoying. I had to speak up or I'd be viewed as foolish. The purpose of our work is to bring our attention to the problems that plague our society.

7. Avoid discussing the show during its airing. There will be a lot of thoughts about the program when you watch it because comedy is so powerful art. After the show, be sure to preserve them before releasing them to the free world.

8. Don't forget to turn off the ringer. Did you really buy a new phone?

9. Be careful not to interrupt. It is possible that you are humorous. Perhaps you've a profession in comedy. It could be that you're awestruck at the level of someone else's. Be careful not to remove the brakes of the racer to determine whether they're still winning. It is likely that you'll be a victim of this.

10. Buy the proper tickets. You must ensure that you watch what you love as comedy is a vast variety of styles. Do not critique Bill Burr for being too angry, Kathy Griffin for being excessively gossipy, Chris Rock for being too controversial and Carlos Mencia for making too numerous jokes that resemble to the ones of Bill Burr, Kathy Griffin and Chris Rock.

11. Be careful not to take offense in the event that you wish to. Every joke is aimed at you have chosen to go to a COMEDY show. It's a shame when you are laughing while another person is being an innocent victim, and then get angry at the time it's your turn. Sometimes, comedians are racist jerks that incite hate and intolerant. So, instead, buy a

ticket for a show by one of the numerous great comedians.

Chapter 4: Each Area Has Its Own Distinct Impression

People who are older, younger, hipper or just plain dumber If you don't know about the difference, then you're not being a good a comedian. Your material should be adapted for the crowd you're hoping to please even though you may have an impressive performance. In all honesty, I'm not really like this. I like telling jokes according to how I think they are amusing If I didn't believe that I had the ability to evaluate humor better than any other person I am not sure I would be brave enough to entertain an public.

But, this is an wrong method. It was not your intention to attend. People don't like pandering however, you may need to do it if you wish the people you meet to smile.

On stage, even most skilled comedians sometimes fail. When you perform comedy at an industrial bar. there's a mistake in the joke the wording is wrong or the stage did not work and so on. There are many reasons it is not possible to succeed in making someone laugh and the comedy will depend on what you do in those instances. Three comics I spoke with on the topic suggested "handling failing" as their solution to failure, and this is certainly an appropriate response.

Anyone wouldn't be enthralled by the notion of having a bunch of fellow revelers laughing along with each other, paying on them, looking forward to each word to receive laughter. It has always been our belief that humor is an extraordinary skill that could alter any conversation to the right direction, or alter the atmosphere and tone of the people close by. It is no doubt that humor is among the most efficient tools of communicating, so it is not surprising that comedians get very rich!

1.) Discover the reasons that you're looking to be amusing?

Like every other time, we start by asking the fundamental inquiry: Why do you Want to Do It? What do you hope to accomplish by doing this? Do you wish to attract your attention? Are you looking to shift your topic to be boring to one that makes an enthralling sensation? Are you interested in using humor in a way that conveys the message while inspiring the audience to consider their own ideas? Do you want to enjoy a great time? Why do you think this is the case? this?

2.) The unique contextual factors

"Of course, I like being the center of all attention. I enjoy having the attention of people who stare at me with anticipation of laughter out loud. I also am a sucker for laughter that is big due to each and every one of my words," the speaker said.

Could this be one of the reasons you choose to make fun of yourself? Well! If so it's possible to think about a few different concerns.

3.) What is the maximum distance you are willing to go to make people laughing?

Well! I'm pretty sure that it is all the extent that is possible, when you're trying to act like a comedy. This is a good choice and it fits the style, so go for it! However, if you'd like to engage in intelligent discussions and employ humor in your everyday interactions, you're looking for an easy explanation to make people smile and change the subject matter and break the ice or simply to help the person you are talking to feel relaxed. That is you're thinking about subtle ways to entertain others as well as an excellent method of gaining control over your situation.

4.) How are you planning to make yourself amusing?

The first step is to determine who you would like to be. A stand-up comic or Charlie Chaplin have different approaches and audiences. Therefore, you must determine which you want to appeal to. If you're a comedian or someone who is known for having a sense of humor and office gatherings featuring you are fun and enjoyable, is contingent on the message that you intend to communicate to people.

5.) Who would you like to mock?

But it can make a difference in what the topic of your conversation will be when you use humor to improve the quality of your conversations and are a skilled communication expert. It's easy to find an idiot on which you base your jokes the majority often time. While it might seem funny at first, and go against the natural instinct to mock this person, be aware that making fun of someone else could result in being judged as a negative person.

It will not reflect well about you if you choose to make jokes about those who are less powerful and able. It is important to know that there are certain restrictions in the event that you use humorous chats.

6.) Jokes that you make up on yourself

Interactions that are non-judgmental, safe, and prevent your from having to face more judgments are the ones where you are most comfortable displaying your incredible funny sense. If you're thinking of going one step further and using derogatory terms ensure that you are using the words against yourself. You can make fun of your actions and errors, in addition to oneself. This does not show how insignificant you feel, but it shows that you're competent to laugh at the mistakes you make and shows you've learned from the mistakes. It's also a lot easier to be a good friend when you're transparent about your flaws.

Everybody can laugh at an innocent person however, it requires courage to laugh at you!

7.) Your tone

Every form of communication such as humor, music and even theatrical performance, concentrate on the diversity in the tone you use. It's really easy to make people go to sleep by approaching this issue on the same tone.

The ability to alter your style, especially when using humor, can have a positive influence on the audience, regardless of whether it was your goal.

8) Understand your audience

Pick your guests, your message and the time you speak. There is no way to criticize a poor decision at a public gathering and explain that it's hurting people. You need to have some shrewdness and be able to comprehend the audience.

9) Rumors

Spreading lies about someone just to garner laughter seems to be an easy thing to perform. Be aware that it can come back to hurt you. And when it does, it will smack your body very hard. Do your best to avoid negative comedy as much as you can. Jokes regarding politics, caste races, or colors is a complete not-to-be-do. There must be professionalism into your comedy if you are not looking to be seen as someone that is not funny.

10.) The imitation of another

It is a great talent for imitating people. This is a fantastic method to use when you are talking. However, you should not use the ability to mock those who aren't there. In the case of him doing it right directly in front of me I did not mind very much. However, when he made the mistake However, when he was doing it in my absence, I was filled of resentment that, even today I am hesitant to speak to him. The kind of jokes that he used to make are not as sophisticated and it is not a good idea to play the role of that individual.

11.) The subject is changed

It is easy to stay with something that is working well, and you want to continue with the same approach as you've achieved a point of success in the event that you discover the audience has been captivated by the topic of your choice. Be sure to mix the topic; a fantastic sense of humor won't happen when you focus upon one topic.

12) Doing a joke about one's appearance

It's okay to mock the behavior of someone else because they don't seem particularly upset at the act. However, you can get yourself in trouble if you are making the mistake of making fun of someone's look, appearance or talents. They are all essential to their identity. You are allowed to have fun however it's better to set boundaries in case you end up turning him into an enemy to be feared.

13) Singing around with everybody, however you

I've met some persons who seem to be hilarious However, after spending short time with them, one gets an impression that they're selfish. There's nothing in their humor. They're entertaining enough. But, they don't realise that, by attempting to make themselves funny the other person, they're demeaning them to boost their own importance. This is totally wrong and causes an opposite impact.

You can be a larger man and be a snarky yourself if you have fun with somebody else. If you are more prone to doing it then you'll gain more respect, not only laughter. We all know that it's hard to think about each word you speak however I strongly advise not to do similar things. As it's hard to be able to make a decision prior to speaking, comedy, as with all kinds of expression, has to be fresh and have its own path so that it can be appreciated by your public.

Do not cover up your feelings by showcasing your humor.

If you are faced with challenges when life gets tough, humor may keep you strong. There are occasions where humor can be harmful which is why it's employed to escape unpleasant emotions, rather than dealing with the issue. Laughter may serve as an escape from emotions aren't something you wish to experience or don't know which emotions to speak about emotions like hurt and fear. or disappointment.

Beware of humor that is sarcastic. It can be effective for certain comedians. However, when used on a personal level, it's not going to be a success but it can also damage the relationship between you. When used as the result of a joke, offensive or obscene words can have the possibility of driving your partner away, and weaken your bond.

Construct inner jokes. One joke that only two of you share will be an in-between joke. It can be reduced down to one sentence or a short expression that reminisces the most humorous or enjoyable stories for the two of you and almost always is sure to make your partner smile or laugh. It may help build intimacy and bond you in the event that only two persons have "in" with the joking.

Perspective from research: people who are funny have the greatest success in their lives

1.) Don't be afraid of failing In the absence of taking chances in life, you will never be successful. It's a fact that we all have but you may not be aware that funny people are more likely to risk it than the average. Every time you hear someone make a humorous observation, they run the risk of making an untrue joke since not all jokes are funny to others (see for instance "Why is some jokes more entertaining in comparison to others")

2.) Thinking about the unimaginable: The most surprising twists are an essential element of a lot of great comedy. Many people are surprised and delighted at this unexpected surprise. The need for creative thinking lets you think outside the boundaries to create unexpected funny comments.

3.) We are all aware that no one laughs with the same laughs therefore this score on social intelligence is quite very high. Actually, some consider jokes annoying. Due to his capacity to watch people closely and know how they behave one who can manage to convey the most effective joke for the appropriate people is usually extremely intelligent (see for instance "Why people are able to laugh at jokes that prove their opinions").

4.) Unique way of living The jokes often take unpredictable turns and can reveal the writer's ability to be creative and innovative. An individual who is funny will not be a part of the masses or conform to traditional social conventions. This allows them to be more successful in his life when he works through it in a proper manner (see for instance "The The psychology of humor").

5.) Since everybody is aware You may think that the majority of people do not know those factual facts, but I've got some good news for you that the majority of people make these inferences regarding a funny person, while not knowing they're the fact that they are doing it. People gravitate towards those with a great sense of humor due to the fact that they have a subconscious belief that they are smart and innovative which is what I discussed in the book "How to convince someone to be drawn to you."

Based on research, laughter improves perceptions of competence prestige, and confidence which makes people who are hilarious extremely powerful. Humor entices people, aids in communication, and encourages education. It's an effective instrument that many successful leaders use in order to boost company the culture of their organization and to build cohesion among employees. If we are more engaged in our work environment and the better our work is, and more likely to suffer from burnout in accordance with studies on positively-run organizations.

Chapter 5: Humorous Types

An uplifting chuckle will make your feel happier in and outside by exchanging numerous chemicals throughout your body. These facts are enough to convince anyone who aren't funny of the importance of laughter. If you're still in doubt, look through these humorous examples for help in deciding.

1. The joy of laughing at your life moments

This specific kind of humor is usually associated with being a bit casual with yourself. If you're blessed with this type of humor, then you are aware of when you should breathe deep and let the tension melt away. There's also a good possibility that you're a friend whom people with a lack of humor seek out for support and love.

2. Ironic Jokes

If you're sarcastic, you've got a brutal humorous sense of humor and probably have had to be told you're offending previously.

You may be a risk to make a statement without thinking about it since sarcasm can be associated to being funny. Your success will be evident when others get used to your specific kind of humor. Be aware of your words before you write when you're trying people to get to know you or what to write in a professional email.

3. Humorous Self-Deprecation

The humor I'm seeing reminds me of many times of the humor that is laugh-at-life and you're always the main character. You love being the school clown, but doing too much can make others get nervous. There's a distinction between a dark comedy and dull darkness.

4. Witty Jokes

The essence of this humor will make your jokes look smart. You're aware of subtle references in films as well as novels. You try to make your jokes seem intelligent without coming off as an opportunist.

Sometimes, witty comedy includes the use of humor. If it is used with a cruel tone it could be offensive to other people. However, when it is handled with care, it is amusing without implying disrespect to others. Your tone as well as your use of humor are crucial elements in sarcasm.

When you tell someone in the office that they have left the car's lights on then they say, "Perfect, just what I was hoping to hear about this day of joy," the person could yell in response. The person is using sarcasm in order to convey that they're having a terrible day. It's just that they're not feeling much of a problem, but that isn't a sign that they're angry at the way you treat them.

5. Toilet humor

The person you know has poop humor when they've sent your a poop emoticon way often! They consider it the most hilarious thing they've seen, even if it's graphic or bloody or just marginally inappropriate. While these jokes might be entertaining but there are certain moments and occasions to use crass comedy.

6. A bit of humor

This is a significant one. It is a type of laugh that you direct away from another person in their direction. Stress and frustration are dissolved by laughing with your friends. It can be an extremely therapeutic and transformative occasion.

7. Dry wit

A person who can express an idea bizarre and hilarious with a calm, unassuming style is referred to for its dry humor.

8. Physical humor

The most straightforward way to express the message is the one that is easiest to convey. The physical aspect of humor is employed. The body has been making excessive or erratic movement of their body. There may be humorous jokes, practical jokes and even gags, however they're usually related to the body, or are centered around the body's movements in an unusual manner. Many people suffer injuries due to slipping or falling, or getting struck by objects falling. Although it can make us laugh, it can be a painful experience to watch.

9. Absurd comedy

The kind of humor that is shown is evident within "Alice in Wonderland" in both a tale as well as a movie. It sifts through the whole world around it and puts it upside down. It's so odd and unique that it turns out to be hilarious - for a few.

10. Improv comedy

Improv is a live theatre kind of performance where the entire comedy is devised spontaneously. It isn't easy to perform an improv show however, often the chaos is the thing that makes it funny. In order to develop the humor an ensemble of performers are required to collaborate. The humour of

Saturday Night Live is frequently made up on the fly.

How is having a great sense of humor essential for success in the world?

It isn't as easy to be being scolded. If you are faced with a difficult situation, the ability to laugh can prove to be extremely helpful. A sense of humor can help you see past difficulties that occur when you interact with people instead of focusing on the negative and becoming angry. Somebody might make a joke of your intentions, like. However, let's face it: often jokes get mistakenly interpreted, and end up being private insults.

Humor helps us avoid taking these incidents as seriously and also to be able to understand the reason the person said or did what they did. There's a chance take part in the conversation if you feel you feel it's appropriate.

Humor can be very important in enhancing relations with others. Making yourself appear approachable as opposed to coming across as uninterested and distant is dependent on a person's sense of humor.

As an example, acknowledging mistakes can be a common element of humour, particularly when someone else has admitted their mistakes. What a pleasure it is to share a moment with a person who shows our humanity instead of trying to convey the appearance of being superior.

This makes people feel comfortable with them if they can use the words "same" or that translates to "I could have done it as well."

A sense of humour can make people a joy to spend time with. We have already mentioned that people who have an innate sense of humor usually appreciate life the way it is instead of adhering to strict ideas. It's like you have a conversation with a person who has an innate sense of humour. This is due to the fact that you're conscious that they won't judge the other person and will comprehend your circumstances. If something isn't going well is also important to maintain a sense humor as it helps to reduce tension and break the frozen ice.

However, the reverse is often the case. It is expected that people who are able to laugh easily are not sensitive when confronted with a difficult situation. The most humorous people are also intelligent individuals. They will help you relax by a humorous yet understanding remarks and are more prone to not overreact in situations that are embarrassing. They learn the art of deceiving and also when it is appropriate to switch their conversation to something more light.

When faced with social situations that aren't familiar in a social setting, humor can be an excellent instrument.

The truth is that people who have a sense of humor are more likely to establish relationships and converse with strangers.

Take into consideration they are able to be funny with other people and cause others to smile. A good sense of humor allows individuals to bond with one another. While it's not pretentious those with a great sense of humor aren't likely to want to be awed by the other. Someone with a great ability to laugh, for example will respond to someone who expresses a love of art with a comment that they also appreciate it, however they "wish they could make greater things that are more complex that stick-men." That's what I'm talking about.

Being able to have a sense of humor can create an environment that's more relaxed that makes it much easier for conversations to flow effortlessly and smoothly with no pressure from either person to be impeccable.

Not least of all, laughter is essential since it's associated with the balance. It is possible to read the emotions of others and be able to respond appropriately by having the ability to laugh. The right balance to strike between serious issues and the lighter ones becomes more enjoyable through a sense of humor.

If you need to, you're capable of mastering formality and seriousness. However, you also can add a touch of beauty and vitality to an area by sharing jokes or jokes with your friends. It's like adding a topping on one's persona to show a great ability to laugh. It helps create a warm and welcoming environment through making people appear friendly and welcoming.

It is common to solve issues in life with humor. The act of laughing at our shortcomings or mistakes is a great way to relax. It can help people feel less anxious and stressed. People find it fun to hang out with funny people.

It's essential to possess an innate sense of humor however, it's equally important to be aware that laughter may lead to issues. It can be difficult for you to surround yourself with people who are funny if you're one who easily gets offended. It is possible that yourself irritated or offended by things others think funny.

The child's ability to laugh may be a sign of their inventiveness and creativity. It is important to think of ways to keep your kid laughing when you see them having a hard time making other people smile or engage in an argument. Making your child a fun name and utilizing it for your own name is a good alternative. Also, make sure you make sure your child is involved in fun activities like films and comedy.

In the case of kids, a ability to laugh is vital. Kids must be taught how to enjoy a great time with their peers and relatives by being funny and entertaining. Your child can benefit by having a laugh and making people smile in social situations and also from learning to develop excellent social abilities. We sincerely hope you enjoyed learning about the importance of laughter in kids. It is essential to have fun whenever you can because it's a fact that laughter is the most effective treatment.

Human brains are an intricate organ. We all have our individual thoughts, feelings perspectives, views, and insight. We all have distinctive experience. We all have an individual sense of humor. There is someone around us who is always able to bring us to laughter or is the most hilarious. Everybody has their own perception of humor. What is considered to be funny is the subject of intensive research.

This kind of humor is loud, combative as well as self-defeating. Slapstick is a type of humor that and even cerebral.

A person who is intelligent should possess an innate sense of humor. Making fun of you, your family members, or even your own activities can make you feel more connected to others as well as reduce stress and make you feel more comfortable in your own skin.

An universal human experience humor is the source of delight, pleasure and even laughter. It's a fundamental aspect of what it means to being human. Humor is a natural ability, for certain people having the ability to laugh at themselves is an essential element of being well.

A positive attitude will help you get through difficult situations or help you fall asleep. It helps in getting rid of anger irritation, anger and negative emotions so that you are able to be happy throughout the day. It also assists in the prevention of conflicts, particularly when it involves people you care about.

It assists in their ability to deal with difficult situations and helps them develop empathy for other people. A positive sense of humor can also teach children to have fun and appreciate the good aspect of things and to maintain a optimistic attitude even regardless of the challenges.

A capacity to be able to smile at yourself and the surrounding world is a vital aspect of an active lifestyle.

It could also prove to be an excellent asset for your child.

An appreciation for humor can assist your child's development into a prosperous and content adult.

Young people need to have a sense of humor as it can make them feel better regarding themselves and others that surrounds them.

The mind of a human being is an intricate organ. We all have our personal thoughts, opinions perspectives, views, and insight. Every one of us has their own distinctive experience. Each of us also has a distinct way of expressing humor. There is someone around us that can never fail to keep us laughing or is the most hilarious. Everybody has their own perception of humor. But, what's considered to be funny has become the focus of extensive studies.

One of the best ways to bring laughter to your professional and personal life is a sense of humor that's tasteful. Furthermore, having a good sense of humor can have many positive effects for your mental and physical wellbeing, since it makes people feel more popular and also attractive.

Individuals with rigid views and appearances are unable to convince others of their worth, and everyone does not have an innate sense of humor. In avoiding harshness, shyness or arrogance, it is possible to increase your ability to do this. These points accurately explain the importance of comedy can be as a talent.

Being a more personable and a person who any person can reach out to help lift spirits, laughter is an excellent way to make the other person in a relaxed mood. Since happy people provide the right amount of charm and pleasure in the monotonous working days with their words and actions driven by a sense of humor people love to chat and collaborate with them.

Negative and gloomy thoughts can be effectively eliminated out of our minds through laughter. In spite of the wild laughter and fun-filled conversations, you'll be able to tackle the problems and difficult events that you could confront in your day-to-day life regardless of whether it's an answer to their problems.

The lightheartedness that comes with optimism keeps negativity off of you and the people surrounding you. Engage with people, smile at the smallest of things and you'll be amazed at how it stops you from spiraling into suicidal thoughts or torturous ones.

Encourages Others

Relaxation is not just a thing you experience with laughter as well, so do the people who are around you. All people face challenges and conflict since these are a part of the normal to the human condition. Most important is to never let these trying circumstances derail your.

Instead, speak to them straight with a smile, make others feel small by using clever humor. Your audience will be impressed and amazed by you having an optimistic outlook that will allow them to deal tough situations with ease.

Enhance your imagination

Based on the latest research, creativity and an innate ability to laugh are linked. Humor is an important skill that helps those with it are able to meet deadlines and achieve goals better. The reason is that laughter eases stress and improves your capacity to make decisions as well as solving issues.

Don't let a stressful situation frighten you, whether you are in a relationship on the job, at the home. Remind yourself and other people that you're not beaten by chuckling or making jokes. The capacity to tackle the problem or finish your tasks eventually will improve.

Maintain your positive attitude to continue burning calories and staying well! The physical and mental health of your body can greatly benefit from laughter since many problems stem from depression. When you laugh or engage in light humor with your friends and burning more calories in your body than any other physical exercise, you can beat and replace negative thoughts with positivity.

The benefits of laughter also boost the immune system through blocking the release of stress hormones. It is no doubt that humor can be a wonderful way to adjust to lead a healthy and healthy lifestyle.

Chapter 6: Maintains Relationships

Humor can strengthen bonds and create trust that can draw people closer. Through constructively sharing smiles and pleasant memories Your connections will grow and grow stronger. The people you meet will be enthralled by them, and relationships and connections with others are bound to grow significantly.

Do not make fun of or mock others under disguise of humor because it causes them pain and causes them to eventually turn away from your company. However the opposite, having a great sense of humor can lead to an enjoyable conversational environment that is built on trust, admiration, and respect.

Harmonizes the people

Being a friendly and approachable person with whom you is able to talk with, and thereby improve the mood, it can be a great way to make others feel comfortable. Because happy people provide an element of fun and charm in the monotonous working days with their words and actions inspired by laughter, individuals like to talk and interact with them.

Many people enjoy laughter as it allows them to release anxiety and enjoy their lives. This is why they are more likely to hang out with people who entertain and humorous.

Helps reduce stress

Every one of us has to cope with tension. A sense of humor will help reduce stress and keep your on the issues at hand.

Health benefits

Laughter is known to improve immune functioning by stimulating your body to produce greater amounts of substances to fight off illnesses. Additionally, it has been proven to relax muscles and reduce blood pressure. It is the ideal method for maintaining your heart's health and decrease the risk of having an attack on your heart.

Helps improve mood

The addition of humor adds the life a flavor and boosts the mood anytime your mood is being shaky because of any situation.

It Benefits Your Brain

It is known that laughter helps the brain is a further benefit that comes from having a ability to laugh. Funny jokes are able to stimulate your brain's area vital for understanding and comprehending.

Improves friendships between friends

If you are able to have fun with a person and feel a sense of connection to you. Apart from having fun and building relationships with people who matter to you, having fun in the company of family and friends makes memories that you'll cherish over a long time.

It helps in calmening anger

It is possible for the situation to become worse If you're angry. It's simple to persuade that people not to notice your faults as well as to prevent becoming annoyed with others while having enjoyable.

Helps others in your area

There is a chance that you can make the people who are around you laugh, and assist people deal with their problems with a good spirit of humor. It is satisfying for you knowing that you have brightened another's day, and assisting those around you in taking time to relax and take in the world.

Creates an impression that is positive

Make a powerful impression when you present yourself like a personable individual, smiling brightly and having a sharp attitude.

Improves the quality of relationships

In addition, laughter is an effective remedy for hurts as well as anger and disagreements. A good laugh can aid you and your spouse navigate the difficult moments within your relationship. The last but not least it improves your relationships.

Another method for getting through the tough moments is to find common interest with people that who you cherish. Also, your outlook gets better when you look forward to that fun moment. Laughter can be a great method to change your perspective and perspective.

Your body is able to experience less stress in performance, as well as increased satisfaction after you smile. Laughter can be a catalyst for change. It could be used as an option in difficult situations when you feel that your existence is meaningless.

The primary source of happiness is laughter. It allows us to let all our troubles in the past, connect with our inner child relax, and take part with one another in a deep connection.

You feel warm in your body and you might have difficulty breathing during times of joy (from having so much fun). There is a possibility of getting 2 hours of peaceful sleep within a few minutes of belly laughing. This has not been achieved with a medication without undesirable adverse side adverse effects.

The ability to detect as well as appreciate the joy of laughter is known as a sense. If you are someone who talks about disasters often and consider yourself a serious person it is unlikely that you'll find laughter in the everyday routines. It is possible to begin by playing the characteristics of a bird. Get used to saying things. Do not be afraid to play off someone else's joke whenever you come across one doesn't everyone can understand.

You can be content even if there is no anyone laughs. When you are trying to become a expert at joking there will be many errors. It is essential to stay with people who are hilarious. Additionally, you could develop your talents through watching hilarious individuals. Make use of these methods to make any debate funny.

The Positive Aspect of Life:

"Your body's reaction to laughter and fun present in your daily life can be expressed by your laughter."

Benefits of Laughter

Having Fun Can Improve Health

Doctors inform us that when the muscles relax after what could an exercise of a minor amount as well, it improves the functioning of your vascular system. The health of your heart improves when you laugh at ridiculous situations. The heart rate rises, as does your blood pressure as you laugh.

Think about the instances where you suffer from a migraine taking in a humorous Netflix show. There is a chance that laughing and watching the show aids in at least a small degree to keep you away from the pain and severity of the migraine. Pain perception does not diminish by distraction alone, but.

The body is increasing its tolerance to pain by following routine procedures. As an example, when endorphins are released, they begin to work. The body creates these natural painkillers due to the fact that the laughter is so intense.

In general, laughter boosts your immune system. This improves your immunity to illnesses. The number of cells within your body which produce antibodies, and increase the effectiveness of T cells when you laugh. 4 In order to fight off disease, T cells function as the army that defends you.

The people who regularly laugh tend to be healthier that the average population. It is normal for blood pressure to rise when you laugh after which it decreases to lower levels, which can benefit overall health and wellness.

The heart muscle as is every other muscle you have the heart benefits from exercising through gaining strength and becoming more effective. When you laugh regularly, it's like joining the heart fitness gym. The research has shown that laughter improves circulation throughout the body, and reduces the likelihood of suffering from heart disease.

Based on research findings that 15 minutes of laughter per day is as good for your heart as exercise for 30 minutes 3 every week.

Chapter 7: Laughter Decreases Stress

Research has shown that laughter reduces stress hormones. If you're under pressure the body produces large amounts of cortisol, which is a major stress hormone. It's essential to decrease cortisol levels as they place stress on the immune system.

There is no way to concentrate on undesirable things simultaneously at the time as you're focusing on something funny. A few laughs will assist you in relaxing and not worrying. It's not even necessary to have that space that you can unwind and breathe deeply can be beneficial.

The humor of laughter can provide a positive perspective. After you've had a laugh, you can find a new method of approaching the issue. Maybe you are reassured by knowing that you've survived previous difficult times. It is possible to see obstacles and challenges as an opportunity by adopting a different viewpoint.

You could also take a look at the positive aspects of the difficult circumstance. It is possible to use humor or laughter as acoping technique if you're embarrassed over something or have to be able to forget an error that you committed.When you're feeling stressed and stressed, the body releases cortisol. Cortisol gets a bad rap since it's considered to be the stress hormone. Despite this, it plays a vital role within the body. Blood sugar levels are maintained, inflammation decreases and metabolism can be controlled and the"fight or flight" response can be activated by your body at the time that it is most needed. When the levels of cortisol are elevated, stress will be perceived by the body.

One method by which the body can help in reducing cortisol levels is by laughing. You get more oxygen with laughter, which increases circulation and reduces levels of cortisol. Based on several research studies, the simple laughter by itself, with no laughter, can help to reduce stress.

The muscles of your body stiffen in the event of pressure. Since laughing can relax your muscles, it may aid in stress reduction. The act of laughing can increase circulation. This can assist in making the muscles relax for as long as 45 minutes.

Finding ways to relax your life and take a break from your own needs may appear as an indulgence, it is essential to your overall wellbeing. Even a 15-minute break every day can prolong your lifespan and allow you to enjoy retirement. In the event that nothing excites you, then just play around and see what transpires.

Being able to have a great time is likely to improve your mood generally. The medical community has discovered that those with a positive view of life tend to do better than those who have an optimistic view of life when it comes to fight against disease. Smile and grin in order for a longer life!

Laughter Enhances Memory

It might surprise you by the fact that comedy has important benefits for your brain. Comedy improves the retention of memories. It is easier to remember the truth more easily if you are presented by a comedian who is appropriate.

Laughter Makes Conversations More Positive

A further benefit for society of humor is the way it encourages greater interpersonal effectiveness.

A person who isn't likely to be interested in talking with you because you've posted an idea or meme. You can have a greater conversation when you use humor, particularly during tough discussions or disputes. One person is more relaxed and the tension diminished.

As well as creating a smile for your relative, friend or colleague smile telling funny stories can enhance their lives. You'll likely leave them happy and in a more positive overall mood than they did.

The whole thing boils down being human and how you interact with other people. There must be a mutual human understanding to be able to laugh at the individual's characteristics, or to make fun of an error that one made.

Laughter increases the quantity of our body's cells which produce antibodies. Furthermore, it boosts the T-cells in our bodies, which are crucial in enhancing adaptive immunity. They assist in the tailoring of our immune system. An improved immune system is a result from all the above. When one laughs, they feel a physical release and a cleansing impact on your body as well as your mind. When people laugh, they are extremely content and as if a heavy burden is removed. When so much is pulling us down, having a laugh at a positive, uplifting way can help.

Bodily release:

Do you remember feeling that you had to have a laugh to keep from crying? Do you feel revived following a lively laughter? It is a form of physical and psychological catharsis.

Internal Exercise:

An enjoyable belly laugh exercises diaphragms, abdominal muscles, and shoulders. It can result in more relaxed muscles afterward. The heart also gets good exercise from it.

Distraction:

As compared to the other seemingly distractions, laughter effectively distracts the mind from frustration or guilt, tension as well as other negative feelings.

In accordance with research on perspective what we do in response to stressful circumstances can vary depending on whether we view the situation as a threat or a challenge. Humor helps us see situations more positively and see them as opportunities, making these situations less daunting and positive.

Social Advantages:

It binds us with the other. Many people think that laughter can be infectious, as is smiling and being friendly. If you can add the joy to your day-to-day routine, you will encourage others to join in and enjoy these benefits.

Feel better whenever you laugh. When the fun ceases, you be happy. In difficult situations, setbacks and losses it is a way to keep a positive, optimistic outlook.

A laugh can be one of the most enjoyable things to do and, in reality, laughter is produced by just being with people you love and your family. The health benefits of laughter are greatly affected by the social aspect. In the absence of taking time with your friends and taking the time to truly be with people, you won't be able to enjoy laughing with your friends.

When you demonstrate to someone that you love them by taking the phone aside and attempting to make contact in person you're participating in a process of rebalancing the nervous system, and reduces defense-related stress responses like "fight or fight." Although you're powerless to alter a stressful situation and you'll both be happier, more positive and more at ease if you have a good laugh.

One of the most efficient methods to keep relationships interesting and fresh is to have fun with each other. Even though sharing a laugh can provide energy, joy and strength, sharing feelings can strengthen and extend relationships. In addition, using laughter to dispel conflict, hatred and hurts is a powerful and effective approach. When times are tough the power of laughter can bring people closer.

By triggering positive emotions as well as the development of emotional connections, laughter and fun-filled dialogue can enrich our connections. The two of us form an intimate bond by sharing laughter. This bond serves as an effective defence against conflict, anger and discontent.

In times of high emotions when emotions are heightened, laughing is the most effective way of dealing with conflict and dissolving tension. It is possible to learn how to employ laughter to ease tensions to ease stress for all who is involved and to make sure that you communicate in a way that improves, not harms your relationships you are with your love ones as well as family and friends and your coworkers.

In boosting the moods of those around you it will reduce their stress levels. You may even be able to have more positive social interactions that will make you be less stressed in general.

Having a Good Time:

There is a way to add some fun to your daily routine by bringing your friends to the cinema or even a comedy nightclub. It is possible that you'll have more fun during the performance that you would normally because of the infectious effects of laughter. Additionally, you are likely to remember jokes from the show later on.

A great place to enjoy happiness and joy can be inviting your friends to an evening of games or a celebration. Setting aside time to enjoy this type of enjoyment can benefit your well-being just like every other routine you follow or even have more fun than many healthy practices.

Laugh More and Have Fun:

Look for humor in your life's difficulties rather than moaning about these issues. Consider the possibility of "look at the past and laugh" when something happens to be extremely frustrating or annoying that you think it's absurd. Try to think of a way to laugh at it by imagining how it could be perceived by your friends.

By embracing this attitude You may also find that you're more entertaining and happy, offering the people around you and yourself plenty of things to smile about. If you live your life by having a sense of enthusiasm, that you're less worried about the negative things that happen.

You can make it up however you want to can:

The fake laughter can offer similar advantages to genuine laughter, according to research similarly to smiling having beneficial effects, whether genuine or otherwise. It is impossible for the body to recognize "real" laughter resulting from genuine laughter as opposed to "false" laughter that you purposefully begin to do.

Physical benefits have the same physical benefits however, the first usually produces the second. To get positive effects, grin and act like you are laughing. It could cause genuine smiles and laughter.

There's plenty of choices to laugh in the entertainment business such as in a theater, or at home watching comedy on TV or streaming films.

A show that is just amusing could cause you to be frustrated, however choosing funny movies and TV shows can be a great method to inject some laughter to your day whenever you require it. The sharing of your ideas with friends gives an item to look back on and share within a group.

Participating in activities that are enjoyable for a variety of reasons lifestyle can help in the prevention of burning out. Stressful jobs with unpredictable high expectations, poor-quality work and no acknowledgment can result in feelings of exhaustion. Offering yourself small prizes, or having groups of supportive friends to give each other high-fives when they accomplish goals that otherwise be unnoticed are two ways I've suggested to alleviate this kind of stress at work. Making sure you get a consistent dose of pleasure and sharing it with your friends can help you do it.

Healthy relationships: Couples who often enjoy each other and explore new activities together could develop an even stronger bond as opposed to when they were stuck in the same rut.

It can be a great way to find someone new to connect with if want to start a new relationship.

Women are more likely to laugh 125% more than men, and guys love women who smile when they are around them.

An innate sense of humor is essential to maintain your relationship in a positive way when you're currently dating somebody.

Positive Mentality:

A regular dose of fun will help you to deal with all the challenges that arise in your daily life. Through this it can change your perception of the stresses within your life and make yourself less prone to stress when it occurs.

Laughter spreads quickly. If you can add some humor into your lives and you can help others follow suit. It is possible to lower anxiety levels of the people who are close to you by boosting their moods. This can increase the number of social connections you enjoy with them. Moreover, lowering your stress even more!

When you are sharing laughter with your friends is the greater chance that they will be able to remember the positive feelings and vibes that you share. Even your close friends are benefited by laughter. It boosts the happiness of relationships and improves their overall.

It is possible to join my group here. Here, you will be able to laugh in a relaxed and safe setting. Laughter clubs can be found all within reach.

The effect of laughter on the body is similar to the effects of deep breathing as it forces the lungs to release much more oxygen than they absorb. This can benefit patients suffering from respiratory ailments such as asthma.

It might not be feasible to lose weight by laughing but a good laughter boosts heart rate and boosts metabolic rate. Try incorporating laughter health into your fitness routine when you're trying to lose weight. It is possible to have a good laugh for 20 hours or more while watching the right sitcom.

It's been proved that laughter can reduce physical discomfort. Along with alleviating pain, laughter creates endorphins with a positive effect on the body, which can be more powerful than equivalent quantity of the opioid. Since more and more people are conscious of the effects that laughter has on your body, the idea of healing with laughter has attracted lots of attention lately.

The release of endorphins following only 15 minutes of laughing increases the tolerance to pain by around 10 10%. The endorphins provide an euphoric "high" which can trigger relaxing feelings and temporary pain relief.

Recent research has revealed that older people who exercise laughter are more optimistic of life. They are also more likely to live for longer than those who tend to be optimistic and down about life.

What's great is that it can make you laugh and encourages you to be more positive. Actually, it's hard to be both gloomy and happy simultaneously. time.

Thus, the next time you're feeling that the glass of yours will be more likely to have half empty rather than filled, you should find something to laugh about, and prolong your time in life.

Chapter 8: The Benefits Of Humor At The Workplace

1. Laughter boosts productivity. According to a study of over 2,500 employees 81% of those who participated stated that they are more productive when they work in a relaxed working environment. The humor of laughter eases stress. Even though they face the same amount of workplace challenges "those who are able to sense humor experience lower stress levels and less anxiety than people with an unsatisfactory spirit."

2. The laughter of laughter can help prevent burning out. Humor is recognized as a way to communicate and, if utilized correctly can help avoid burnout and improve stress resilience.

3. Humor can be a source of inspiration. The application of humor to the workplace is linked to increasing morale among employees and promoting a positive corporate culture and increasing the motivation of employees.

4. The size of your paycheck increases with the amount of humor. That is that the more fun the bosses were, the more lucrative their rewards were. Their bonuses was directly proportional to their use of humor.

5. Brain power overall is enhanced with the joy of laughter. When you laugh, the serotonin chemical in the brain to be released. It improves the cognitive process generally and improves attention and objectiveness.

6. Laughter enhances decision-making. Positive emotions can lead to more flexible making decisions, an increased variety of activities to search for, and a higher level of analytical rigor.

7. Acceptance of concepts that are new can be boosted through humorous interactions. Unique interactions help individuals to provide new concepts.

8. Humor can spark new connections. Humor is a great way to encourage new thinking

when it comes to design or problem solving classes.

9. Ability to tackle problems is enhanced by humor.

Watching comedies may boost the capacity of a person to think creatively when solution, as per research.

10. Humor engages listeners. The audience is more inclined to take note of or to listen to what you convey if you use appropriate humorous language often.

11. It is believed that laughter can improve memory retention. Clarity behaviors--instructional messages that draw students' attention and aid them in understanding the course material--improve students' capacity to process the material, which increases retention and learning.

12. Persuasion is aided with comedy. "When you are delivering a message is not popular, humor could be very persuasive since it prevents them from making counter

arguments, for instance, since they don't believe that it's being forced in their faces."

13. Laughter is a great way to boost learning. The research has shown that using humor in a class can reduce anxiety, create a comfortable environment and accelerate the process of learning.

14. Humor makes people likable.

The innocent humor of people makes them likable and appealing to each other.

15. Humor can make us feel more social. Positive sound effects can trigger an emotional response in the person listening's brain. This could be laughing or shouting "woo hoo!" This automatic response causes us to smile or laugh. It makes us feel more connected to others and enhances social interactions.

16. Humor is a way to connect people.

"Humor is regarded as an important social asset and, when utilized with care it can bring to the person who is presenting an active interest and the gratitude of other people. Through displaying shared feelings and alleviating tensions, sharing laughter brings intimacy, connection and bonds of friendship.

17. The differences in status can be lowered through the humor.

The barriers between management and their employees is easily bridging through humor.

18. Laughter builds confidence. "Negotiators are more likely to have greater relationship trust, higher mutual gains and greater satisfaction with the process as well as their partners" as they begin online transactions with humorous interaction.

19. The spirit of collaboration is encouraged by humor.

Based on a growing amount of research, laughing is a mirroring of not just one's facial expressions but also nervous and hormonal activities which can lead to an increased desire to be healthy and well.

20. The use of humor can enhance the way leadership capabilities are perceived. "Whether or not they're really in control or in charge, individuals who use humor, particularly during stressful or possibly impossible situations, are perceived as a leader who is in control of things, having authority and able to take control.

21. Humor can help resolve conflicts. The concept of humor has been viewed for a long time as a powerful equalizer and a means that helps to build relationships and bridge gap. Actually, humor has been proven to be a key element of the process of international mediation and peacebuilding.

22. Opportunities are created through the use of humor. Based on research, executives who have a great sense of humor receive many more chances in their organizations over those who are not.

23. Humor boosts credibility. "Users who are humorous are regarded as being more credible and competent."

24. Laughter raises ratings.

Humor in supervisors is associated with better work efficiency of subordinates and satisfaction. It also improves evaluations of performance by supervisors, workplace cohesion. It also has been linked to less quitting.

25. Humor improves coping skills. "People have the ability to transform negative situations into positivity, thereby making them more able to deal difficult situations and by recognizing humor when they are in dangerous or stressful circumstances."

26. The immune system is strengthened through humor.

Through reducing the production of stress hormones such as cortisol as well as increasing the production of immuno-enhancing substances like beta-endorphin, laughter can boost immunity.

27. The effects of humor help muscles relax. "Humor boosts the immune system reduces blood pressure and helps relax muscles."

28. Laughter is a great way to burn calories.

"Liking things 100 times a day can burn just as many calories as riding on a stationary bicycle for 10 minutes."

29. Humor makes people happier.

30. "One of the most beneficial ways to be happy in your life is to have humor.

The type of humor you choose to use is essential if you wish to make use of it successfully. Different types of humor, like can produce drastically diverse results in classroom settings.

Positive humor has been linked to higher learning results An informal learning environment and better assessments for students and motivation for learning as well as better information retention as well as higher levels of satisfaction.

Negative humor, specifically targeted at particular students or a group of students has been associated with poorer results in learning, a tense classroom environment, less satisfactory assessment of students, higher levels of distractions as well as lower levels of satisfaction.

Similar developments have been noted across other areas like work management. These trends have been observed in other fields, such as the effect of both positive and bad comedy. That's why it's important to choose a comedy style that's appreciated by the public, while staying clear of humor that is not viewed positively as it could work against the goals you're trying to achieve.

Although it may be difficult to differentiate between two types of humor, it's generally recommended to stay in the direction of prudence and avoid any jokes that you think your audience might find offensive or insulting.

Keep in mind that the appropriateness of a joke is contingent upon the circumstances and people you're speaking to. A joke, for instance, appropriate for sharing with your people who are drinking in the bar might not be appropriate for sharing with students in a class.

It is the humor's design that counts for the effectiveness of a joke.

Specifically:

In general, gentle humor can be the most efficient. In terms of enhancing the memory of people, for example moderate humor is often able to perform better than serious humor. Sometimes, minor humor, such as the clever use of a pun, may help in boosting memory. In excess or inappropriate humor, it can cause various problems that can affect others' perceptions of your character.

Generally speaking, laughter is most effectively when it's too subdued. The use of extreme humor is generally not a good idea, however it is also advisable to avoid be humor that is not subtil because people may be unable to detect it. This can make it uneffective.

The best kind of comedy is determined by various factors such as the environment as well as your audience similar to the kind of humor that you employ. In some situations, you could make sure your audience will be receptive to a gentle comedy, however, not necessarily to overt humor however in some instances there is a chance that people won't be able to grasp the humor at all.

In the case of using humor in particular in order to bring interest to information or enhance memory of the information there are several aspects to be considered along with the above rules that serve as general guidelines for how to effectively use humor:

In general, any humor relevant to the topic at hand will be more successful. Choose a suitable comedy and in particular, one that connects specifically to the points you are trying to communicate. If it's unexpected in a certain way, it can help viewers pay attention and retain the facts more easily. Therefore, you should try to avoid facts which your viewers might think are too predictable.

Chapter 9: How To Pleasantly Upset Your Audience

This chapter will focus on the basic elements of humor as well as the reasons and methods of having fun. If you're not keen on the theory of humor and want quickly get to the practical aspects of becoming humorous, you might prefer to skip to chapter 2.

Laughter is the body's psychological and emotional reaction to a threat that is not armed. To illustrate, let me give you an example which occurred a couple of days back.

A former college friend from my college days, Lisa, was visiting my house for dinner. We were able to talk about past times and other things when, after having completed eating,

Lisa went to the toilet. Then, a second after I heard a shrill screaming, and I ran out to meet Lisa on the toilet in a state of shock as she saw a massive spider in front of the trash can. I realized that it was not a real spider Halloween toy that my niece has played with earlier (and I tried to get rid of it when she went out - but it turned out that she had missed the trash bin) I opted to take part with the intention of being amusing.

I instructed Lisa to remain put I rushed back to the kitchen, and bought the Jar. After returning I acted as if I was trying to catch the spider using the jar. In the process, I made use of the edge of the jar in order to alter the spider to appear as if it were moving, this made its capture challenging. Then I let out a pained yell, shouting "It was a biting me! It was able to escape!" which only caused Lisa to get even more scared as she nearly fell off the bathroom seat. Then I looked up at her, smiled and then stood the fake spider up for her to observe the fake spider wasn't actually a threat, and it was just a fun Halloween prop.

It was this realization that prompted her to let loose a wild and inexplicably excessive joy. Even as hilarious as I consider that I am, the laughing was not a result of my act. The reason for her laughter was purely due to the emotional feeling of relief she received after realizing that the danger that triggered this whole thing was neutralized; that it was not in fact there. This is a way that laughter could be an act of relief from a dangerous situation.

If you're having a difficult time understanding the way jokes are framed as threats, you can consider the idea within relation to Jay Leno's infamous "Headlines" segment. It's the part that the host. Leno reads newspaper headlines that contain hilarious misspellings, grammar mistakes, or even atypical expressions like "Reeding tutors required" or "Weight increase made Butt to stand out." The reason why the segment is hilarious is due to the fact that these headlines were extracted from a real printed newspaper (usually the newspaper). The segment is a bit of fun because Leno provides us with physical newspaper clippings. If he did not show us the actual evidence it wouldn't be able to be funny to us. Consider it this way. If there was no physical proof that we have, we would not be compelled to accept a challenge to the way we think of a newspaper as an eminent entity, brimming with talented editors and writers as a model of grammar appropriateness and neat phrasing, giving us the most important information of the day. It's the infringement of the preconceived ideas about what a paper should be that reveals the absurdity of "Headlines." The reason for viewers to respond with joy, rather than fear or worry is the basic confidence that these bizarre headlines on news stories, while disturbing they aren't threatening. They're just fake spiders lurking in our garbage cans.

The art of comedy is of playfulness and disruption. If you wish to get people laughing, it is important to look for cracks in their assumptions and break them up with a manner that's provocative but never threatening. A lot of people do this with humor that is sarcastic and deadpan.

Sarcasm can be described as the silly (and in the case of misuse or misused, even snooty) affirmation of seriousness the subject in apparent disregard of someone else's expectations or expected perception. If a child doesn't enjoy broccoli can be seen as sarcastic when the mother tells him playfully (or in a snooty manner) "Yeah Mama Let's eat broccoli every the night during this time. Let's plant some broccoli in the backyard when we're done." If you're looking to get people laughing using sarcasm, a well-placed joke is an effective technique.

The essence of deadpan humor is an expression of sarcasm, with the "dead pan" delivery. Deadpan is essentially about a dull voice, and a look of apathy. Deadpan humor can be a bit confusing to people since they're never certain that you're actually joking. This is, except for Andy Kauffman, can be somewhat confusing. One excellent illustration of deadpan humor could be seen in the Ben Stein appearance in Ferris Bueller's Day off. Ferris Bueller is absent from the roll call for attendance and Stein's monotone voice, "Bueller, Bueller" as well as the silence that follows is legendary.

Chapter 10: Don't Be Afraid To Be Un-Funny

Are you in a classroom or meeting, and noticed another person is making everybody smile? Worse of all you can see that they're doing it with almost the same joke that was already in your head but you were too afraid to speak it out.

The two things, being funny and shy are not compatible. Someone who is funny is loud and takes risks. It's not necessary to be someone who has a tendency to dominate conversations. Also, you shouldn't be perceived as someone who is who is trying to make others feel like you. However, you do need to be on the market and be prepared for an uncomfortable silence after an idea you thought was hilarious is ignored. Funny people take advantage of their moment with no hesitation. If it's something like humor that is as elusive as it gets, you can always analyse your approach to the attempt of being humorous. Do not fall into the trap of over-analyzing. Your audience should perform the analysis, and return with a "funny oui" decision. There is nothing wrong with your efforts.

The "DO NOT ABORT" Rule:

One good general rule is to finish and express fully your thoughts when you start to express them. Also when you've thought about or in your subconscious, processed an idea to the degree that your brain has stimulated the mouth to work toward vocalization Don't stop! Do what you can to keep it going. Comedy is the antithesis of a politician, given the sense that comedians minimize self-censorship.

Recalling what was stated in the intro The normal and expected experience of professional comedians that they fail (or to completely bomb) in their initial attempts at entertaining the audience. That's fine. Even at a more informal stage, becoming a humorous person demands the willingness to take on failures in humor. If you persist and persevere through the rough spots the reward is very worthwhile.

Chapter 11: Timing And Delivery

In the writing process, comedy demands an understanding of how humans take in information. To get people laughing, it is necessary to develop an understanding of what information is perceived and interpreted by the viewers. The use of rhythm, speed and the tempo of a comedic performance to improve its delivery.

A simple, yet overlooked element of comedy timing is the pausing. To get people laughing it is important to know where you can and when to stop your speech. A pause can be employed to allow the audience the chance to digest details to set up. When your joke involves performing an acrobatic or impromptu play with words it is utilized to provide the audience with time to think about the comedy together and "get the concept." People love the challenge of having to do a little (not excessively) and "get" the gag. They feel a sense of ownership in the comedy and the laughter of the audience will not only be a sign of approval and validation of your comic creativity, but of their own.

The use of pauses is also in order to build suspense prior to an action. Imagine you've got an extremely funny story of your last dental visit that is a great short paragraph that summarizes your own unique perspective on the entire experience. The description of your visit will serve as your introduction and the tale should entertain viewers by it by providing a believable and fascinating narrative. Before you start the one-line punch line take a break for a second.

"I have paid the charge and was about to leave when I picked the horrible taste of battery acid inside my mouth. I noticed one lady waiting in the room. It was my opinion that I must be able to warn that woman."
.....Pause ......

This pause is going to leave your audience waiting for the punch line/one-liner.

The ability to time your speech can be put to good use when you are cognizant of the speed of your communication. Certain phrases should be spoken rapidly, whereas others are more deliberate. If you're looking to be humorous, you shouldn't rush through your jokes or give an impression that what you're telling isn't important or interesting. But if you have some reason that warrants using rapid delivery to diminish the importance of an element in your comedy or routine or routine, then take it. An excellent example of fast-paced delivery is George Carlin's well-known "Seven words You Shouldn't Use on Television" routine, in the course of which he deliberately and continually accelerates through repetitions of seven "dirty words" that can't be used in public broadcasting and slows his speed down with an in-depth review of the reasons why these seven words aren't so bad as some of believed.

The timing of comedy is vital for slapstick and physical comedy. A bucket of water rarely gets to Charlie Chaplin's head until that ideal moment.

Chapter 12: Where To Get And Not To Get New Material

One of the best ways to make your life more entertaining is to increase the range of your personal encounters. The more diverse and unique your experiences, the broader perspectives on your life that you'll be able to examine. Don't fret about it, in a humorous sense knowing all about life in the modern world isn't that hard. You're looking to discover things that a majority of people have experienced and have knowledge of. This helps you more effectively connect with your readers. As an example, the experiences of being a couple, having a spouse, girlfriend or children are all quite common, simple and everyday situations that let you discover the common "funny" basis to connect with your people who will be watching if you opt to incorporate certain of these stories within your topic.

Another excellent place to start is with pop culture. Some people don't like reading Hollywood gossip sites however, some people do. If you're among those folks, you'll appreciate the "research aspect" of being a comic. You must soak everything you can, including the latest news, trivial information as well as every ounce of pop culture nonsense that comes from the sewage. You'll be current and filled with interesting material that audiences love to laugh over.

When you are looking for fresh material, pay attention to what you learn from comedians who are not yours. Don't wish to get found when you are in an informal context, imitating another's routine without crediting them. For jokes that are simple it's more original. They lend themselves to trading, borrowing and sharing. But do not try to pass off personal stories and routines you've created which aren't yours without acknowledging their source writer. It's fine to be a bit naughty; it's okay to be inspired by comedians of other genres and take bits and pieces of their material in your own. But at the time of writing it is supposed to be your own. The effect will be much more natural in this is the case and ultimately you'll be more entertaining for it.

Chapter 13: Tap Into A Continuous Stream Laughter

The campfire game is a classic which perfectly illustrates the infectious spirit of laughter that can be found in groups.

Participants gather in a group in front of the fire. The game starts by two players sitting side-by-side to one another, each selecting an animal, and then trying to imitate the animal. Participants make guesses about what animals they are imitating. If a player guesses which animal is correct, they is required to mimic the same animal in laughter (the one that he has guess correctly, for instance for example, a goat that is laughing). Once the animal of the first participant has been identified, she ceases her performance and the person who is to her left starts to mimic an animal that she has chosen. If someone isn't already performing an animal's imitation continues to guess (usually with a hysterical laugh) until just one person remains who is not performing imitating a laugh-version of the animal.

What you'll find with this game is it doesn't reach its planned final stage. In most cases, after that third player try to replicate the laugh of a goldfish or Giraffe, the whole scene transforms into a roaring, unstoppable explosion of laughter.

Like fire, humour has a self-sustaining nature and requires just a constant source of fuel to sustain it. If you want to inspire people to laugh it is important to understand how to nurture this self-perpetuating environment. Here are some suggestions:

Relax and enjoy:

Maintain a cheerful, positive and cheerful mood throughout your social settings. It's possible to do this by being a happy and cheerful person who doesn't take his life too seriously.

Make Sure Your Own Laugh is Cheerful and Not Distracting:

A few people are cursed with an obnoxious laughter. If you're not cautious, the laughter you have can turn into its own, ad-libbed punchline. If you're laughing in a way that could cause Fran Dresher chuckle it's best to try control it a small amount. Practice makes perfect.

Be Confident:

The confidence you have is a key factor to enhancing your imagination and expressing your humorous views of life in a manner that people naturally desire to react. Also, confidence is essential in the creation of self-deprecating humor, which doesn't cause uncomfortableness.

Be Selective About Your Environments:

If you're nursing, or medical professional, then you're probably not going to want to invest too much time trying to make a joke in the discussion of the rapid expanding cancer that is that is affecting the lymph nodes of the patient who is in room 202. However sketches of an MD who is trying too hard to make a joke when it's not the right time can be a great hit. In general, however it is important to recognize the venues that allow you to make a splash at the event, and also other places in which you should keep the atmosphere low-key.

Adopt a Mischievous Attitude:

The most important term used in comedy is the "target or object being mistreated during a comedic show. They could include audience members as well as celebrities, shopping malls or your personal weight problems or anything else that is really. An excellent comedian tends to poke and poke at the people she is targeting, hoping to find funny gems. So, comedians can get the most from an irreverent attitude, or a fun-loving, impish character looking to stir things up some and maybe get into some troubles. Make sure you exercise care and pay attention to the crowd around. This might not be the most appropriate choice to head into the bar of a biker to try the routine. Start with a group of close buddies at first.

Read and research a great deal of Jokes:

Doctors and lawyers aren't shy about maintaining a folder of jokes on their computers to be used for business events, parties or whatever. One of the easiest and best ways to make yourself humorous is to become an individual who is able to tell hilarious jokes. Jokes can be great at bringing new life into an argument when it's got boring. Jokes are also excellent for getting individuals in a good mood when it comes to sales pitching or negotiations. It's not necessary to recite and memorize the jokes that you've read in order, but learn the basic rules and then try to practice the jokes.

Chapter 14: Man With The Humorous Reputation

If you constantly delight people by your humor and wit and wit, you'll soon develop an image of being hilarious. It will happen only if you are in your own way and do not pretend to be someone else. Most people, especially younger youngsters especially do this. They're amazed by the classmate or friend that constantly cracks everybody up, and wonder what they could do to be similar. They try to emulate this person and discover they can't achieve it in a regular manner.

Funny characters can be found in all kinds of dimensions, styles and shapes. Learn what you're about and in which area you have your best comedy talents. If you're given the chance to network, you should join other comedians and have a chat. Like everything other, it's possible to completely nerd out over comics. Venue, timing, involvement, bombing are the things comedians like to talk about among themselves.

It's also crucial to recognize the darker side of comedy. It is a source of laughter that can be therapeutic and positive, but because of its nature it is a source of negative energy. Comedy has the responsibility for comedians and comedy to challenge the assumptions we make and to look at the world in new and exciting ways. This means dismantling and challenging our current norms. Sometimes, it's also about the vilification of others, regardless of whether or not, even if the attack is just in jest and humor. It's the sinister and proper moral ethos of comedy. A lot of comedians, even more than those in other fields struggle with anxiety and addiction to substances. It's not to say it's impossible to be healthy, happy and charming person however, you should prepare for the possibility of visiting some very darker places along the way.

There's enough to say about the dark side of comedy. Also, it's true that people just like comedians. If you're hoping to make acquaintances or have more dates, having a sense of humor is definitely a benefit. When it comes to dating specifically, having a sense of humour can create a significant difference. The ability to laugh can calm tension such as first date situations, and lets people let down their inhibitions and let loose somewhat. Also that for men, especially having the ability to get the attention of an entire group is viewed by women as something that is attractive.

It's great to get an image of being humorous. This is much more beneficial than the reputation of boring. No joke.

Chapter 15: The Parallel And Opposite Story

They are a lot of amusement. When two or three people are in the same spot in the same place at the same time they'll attempt to compete in telling stories. "You had a catch this large? Oh, yeah. I caught fish that were bigger." They are both two stories that have a bigger conclusion. Once a couple of guys have established the general pattern of the story, it's time for you to write an alternate story which is completely different. If they catch a larger than average fish, you will catch the Sardine. It is important to remain as naive as you can. This is a good illustration. Find staples that could be connected.

Guy 1 It was the summer of 2007. I graduated from my MBA within 18 months. I worked at two different jobs, but I was able to achieve an average of 3.4.

Guy #2 This reminds me of the time I completed my PhD. Within a year and 14 months. I ran my own company, but I got my job completed. 4.0 I'm very proud of it.

They are stories that have parallels. Then it's time for you to share this parallel tale from the other side.

"You Guys, I'm not trying to boast, but I completed my Associates Degree at MCC within a little less than three years. The process was not without sacrifices, however, I was able to get the degree done...at at least for the initial 30 to 40 credits. It was not showboating, but I was an 2.2. I worked for taco bell. By "work there" I'm referring to eating often there.

Keep track of the staples you'll be able to reference. In the case below are: the name of the college, the number of years that it took to obtain the degree, any additional work and the GPA. When you've noted these elements and retelling the story in the reverse is as easy as the word "mad in a lib."

The more self-deprecating and self-aware you can do, the more successful. It's disarming. I'd suggest clarifying you're laughing. You can be able to say, "I'm sure you know that I'm not serious." Make sure to be bold. The more daring, the more effective.

Creatively Positive

If it's simple to tell someone "Jim's stupid he... (insert imaginative insult here) Then it ought to be as simple to state, "Jim's so smart he... (insert imaginative exaggeration here).). Example:

"Hey If you're hitting the numbers that you're hitting you'll all eventually retire. There will be a lot of us swimming in the chocolate-pudding pools as well as riding our own personal rollercoasters to our very own island for a month of vacation."

Be creative not negative.

However, Dave this is so boring, normal and dull. What can I do to create a more enjoyable experience?

Thank you for your question. Yes, I'm planning take the time to respond. (But don't believe that I didn't have an opportunity to offer the solution to a different query.) The best way to take this idea further is to make it sound insulting.

"Great Steve is at work so hard that everyone will receive increments. Work horse. Was your childhood influenced with loving parents? I would like to see you the age of 90. Health Nut."

Take a chance. You're more entertaining than you imagine.

Use a positive, creative approach without a harsh tone.

Sarcastically Encourage a Horrendous Behavior

This method is best used when it comes to the conclusion of a conversation when it is time to say goodbye. Examples: "Have a great day, Bill. Come back tomorrow. Also, don't be late paying your taxes."

It's a fun and lighthearted approach to close the conversation.

If you want to really make it funny, you must do the following three things: 1. Make it sound positive in your attitude as if it's an excellent thing. Talk to your friend in a manner that suggests this behaviour was going on for an extended time 3. Include a particularly devastating explanation to justify this behavior.

Example:

"See you next week, Todd. Don't let your kids be neglected. It is well-known the love of a parent is a weak points. Parents don't want children who are weak are you Todd? Look at me. I had great parents."

The Art of Eves-Dropping

and Butting and Butting

The name of this technique comes from its purpose, "The Art of Eve's dropping as well as Butting into." One safe method to make a joke when working is to reply an unanswered question addressed to you. When Jane as well as Cindy are in close proximity and discussing, for instance an event, drop in and respond to questions they have asked the other.

Before I get started I must address a key part of the tone that I'd like to discuss. It's not difficult to employ this method in a manner which is a bit frustrating. It's been seen in use in a way that isn't right. The effect can go backwards and work against the person you are trying to help. The result could be that you seem like a pro or appear as a self-deprecating non-person who is unable to join in. But the correct method to approach it is to appear a bit annoyed that someone might ask the query. This is an example of this:

Jane and Cindy: "Did you get a dress that you can wear to the wedding on Saturday?"

You're "I did not attend the wedding, but if had, I definitely would not wear a gown. Thank you for asking Jane (really rude). What was your weekend like?

You should give this technique a go. You'll be surprised by what the results of your determination will be.

Answering a Question

If no one is asking you the question, and you are able to answer that question, there's a built into a comedic aspect. However, what should what do you do when been directly asked a question? One option is giving the solution to another question that is different from the question that was posed. I understand what you're thinking. This is just irritating. How can you avoid becoming annoying and instead make it humorous? It's easy, just be condescending, and maybe off-putting with your answer. Example:

James (to Dave): James (to Dave): Dave can you tell me what to do to access the room for supplies? I'm looking for additional post-its."

Dave (to James): "You make a right on Kyrene to the right, then right onto Guadalupe and take a right to McClintock. In the corner to the south there is the Walgreens. The store has a pharmacy, where it is possible to get everything you'll need. In the future, stop touching your hands until you've cleared it up."

In order to make it more funny, you need to be sure to speak very loudly, so that everybody hears it particularly the final phrase.

Anyone would think that this is an extremely unkind thing to say to somebody. This is. What makes it so funny? The reason it is hilarious is because of Fourth wall. It's hilarious to those who are watching. This isn't funny for the person you're talking to. This shouldn't make sense to people they don't know. The problem must be addressed.

This is a major reason why social interactions have become more unpleasant. The art of reflection mirrors reality, mirroring life. Television shows show things and then do them on the ground. People's behavior towards their counterparts on the screen could be incredibly rude. But it's fun for viewers from the other end from the wall to those watching. If we approach people on the street with television behavior, it's ugly. That shouldn't happen. Engaging with people solely to entertain viewers is a talent that should only be used by those you have already gained trust with. This should not be utilized for building a bond. Take care of people first. The difference between the two is comedy intelligence.

Know your audience. Linda Your boss who is listening to this, might enjoy the conversation.

How do you convince those who're exactly on the same page of the fourth wall to have fun? The answer is in the next section.

Self-deprecation Maximization

This is quick and simple. If someone is rude to you, the usual thing to be defensive and then insult them. "You believe I'm a 'this or that, and guess what I believe is a "this or a "that.'"

"Oh I'm sorry, we really will be a certain or another and one."

I have a suggestion for you: the next time you're thrown off instead of reacting defensively and defending yourself, ensure they don't realize the extent to which they're right. Continue to prove them wrong. Show them proof. Between you and me, I'm sure that you'll create something much superior to what you would have by yourself.

If you keep doing this more often, you'll notice how some individuals are absolute fragiles, and they have the ability to serve it well, but are unable to accept it when it comes back. This doesn't mean that you can't return it, it simply implies that there are people who are sensitive. Still, you must interact with those who are sensitive. Try your best, whenever you are able help build those who are sensitive. They tend to be the most protective. However, they could end up becoming the best and nicest all-round friends. Know your audience.

When I was working, it was mentioned that I had smaller hands. I could have been defensive and then reacted, "I don't have small hands. You have large heads," as well as generating funny cleaver jokes about big heads. Instead, I decided to jump on the bandwagon. Small-hand jokes are running for around 4 months. Most of them are my own.

"This keyboard is huge."

(Holding the airport-sized bottle of hand Sanitizer.) "Check out this 10 year stock of hand soap."

"How can it be that there's no sound whenever I clap?"

I have more fun than any other person, and I haven't even put up.

(Insert an appropriate phrase...

instead of ...)

You can make fun of an ad-hoc phrase you've encountered in the workplace by showing the absurdity of the word and link it to the absurdity using the expression "as as opposed to." ..." does it sound complex? The truth is that it's easy and you could apply it to almost anything. This is an example of my work place in which I worked. The most frequently used words I have heard was "to my knowledge." ..." prospective clients will contact me with questions like "How many years will it take to complete the course?" All too often it was, "Too my knowledge it's three years."

There is a place for you to think outside the box during office conversations. "To my knowledge, it's only three years, whereas to Steve's understanding of six years. However, according to me, it's three years."

Chapter 16: Tips To Avoid Politics Using Humor

Do not discuss the politics of workplace. Avoid discussing hot subjects such as religious convictions or personal convictions But, especially I'll repeat it, don't discuss the topic of politics in your workplace. There is a lot of conflict in the workplace. You aren't sure where the others stand. In the end of your day, it is important to cooperate. Making sure that the work gets done is far more crucial than making sure everyone is in the same boat. The key is to be the person to put aside politics. Do not bring it into at work.

Someone is bound attempt to lure you into an argument over the political scene. You should get out. It's fine to tell them, "I don't talk about politics in my workplace," then walk away. If they insist, admit the fact that it's unwise to speak about politics within the office. One could go as you can say "Do you believe I'm stupid enough to allow that in the workplace with mixed company?" If they persist and ultimately you be a target for someone else who is persistent with you, it's rude and also a ploy, don't take it lightly. Invariably, somebody will respond with "So whom are you voting for?"

You can say "I often write with (X famous person, with me as the VP)." I will always declare, "I'm writing for Keanu Reeves...again."

If you're caught up involved in a heated debate, it is possible to get yourself out of the argument with gentle humor. I've utilized this particular tool to end three heated debates. Two colleagues were arguing over the same time over a controversial subject in the political world and attempted to convince me to end the argument. I replied, "You know what really frustrates me? People who are trying to be able to compromise like adults. Take it to the ring. There's a problem. I'm fed up of listening to opposing sides and coming together to seek solutions. Fight. You're both wrong. Correct the other.

Another thought on the subject of politics. Always look for funny jokes that will make everyone happy. In the words of the famous and intelligent Will Rogers, "Don't blame the President. Not is he even aware of the situation."

The Jerry Seinfeld Game

"What's the matter regarding coffee cups? Are they a cup that is made with coffee? No, I'm not sure. Head cheese Wow. It's awe-inspiring. look at those words that are squeezing around." These are genuine comedy from Seinfeld's "I'm telling you this for the final time." The classic comedy of the "Great One", Jerry Seinfeld.

It is possible to use it due to the fact that there are two meanings of the word. A coffee cup may mean the cup was designed made of coffee, or it could mean that the cup is made from coffee. To gain a better understanding of interpreting language, Greg Dean's standup book is unbeatable and is a must-read for anyone who is interested in becoming a comic.

Skip one head, skip one head. I was performing an impersonation scene during an evening class at The Annoyance. I was a very nervous comedian, who was trying the latest jokes to a buddy prior to taking the stage:

"What's to be said about hair ties? Does it come with hair? What's the matter about glasses? Do you have a glass to consume drinks from, made by eyeballs?"

The scene made me want to create a list of compounds and to attempt to come up with a different interpretation of one or both the words, and then combine them in order to explain the new definition or incorporate the definition of the word in a paragraph that will help explain or highlight the absurdity in the meaning that is now given to that compound word.

What is the best way to take part in game Jerry Seinfeld game:

Step 1: Make an alphabetical list of compound words.

Step 2: Search for several definitions of the two terms.

3. Explain the definition of "new"

Step 4. (Optional) Use the word in a sentence that enhances the meaning of the new word.

What's up with coat hangers? They sound like they're killing those who wear rope.

What's with these desserts? What was the date when they began creating beautiful women from Ice cream?

What's the matter about Bundt cake? Shouldn't it be able to take the cake in a complete swing?

What's the matter regarding drawers in dressers? This seems like an option, "Are you going out this evening wearing a dress? Or drawers. Perhaps that's underwear to the dresser.

What's the problem about digital clocks? They'll make you feel with numbers.

What's the issue with slim computers? This is a machine that requires a V8.

What's up about Dry erase board? For seven years, a dry erase board was completely clean.

What's with the ab busters? This is a small vacuum in the stomach. The team could be one which stops abbs from taking advantage of. The abdominal muscles combat crime, a brand new show that airs available on Spike TV. Abb busters 8/9 Central.

I hope you had fun with playing the Jerry Seinfeld game. This is an excellent exercise in writing. It helps to think more creatively. It is recommended to identify compounds that are specific in your workplace or field. You should keep these notes handy to be able to reference them at the appropriate time.

Getting Back to Someone

This method is called "Getting back to Someone." One of the most important things to do when it comes to returning to someone is to contact them regarding something that they did not ask for you to talk to them. The more humiliating the worse. That's similar to what it says. Here's an illustration.

"Hey Geoffrey, I wanted to follow up with me on the matter I asked you about, and you'll find that the answer is yes, there's no coverage for prenatal birth to anyone else than your spouse. We want to be sure of this. This is only valid for relatives.

In order to make it efficient, wait until you have a few people about, specifically the new employees. Establish the mood for an enjoyable office.

Chapter 17: Greatly Exaggerate Your Numbers

This is will be helpful to those who work in a job that is based on numbers which is solely about numbers. It's good to know that it's possible to work within one of those.

If you work in any job that is based on numbers, there will be a time when someone asks questions about your figures. I was employed at a college where the staff would inquire what number of students you were likely to be enrolling every month. It's a good idea to have about four, five or six. That's a boring solution. It is essential to be truthful majority of the time in order to create a great joke. So that you know when it comes time, you can tell when the time is appropriate. instead of stating 4, 5, 6 or 7, use 47. 47 is the most fun number.

"Hey Jason, how many did you get this week?

"Oh, 72. This should be a great week.

The ideal time for this is when you're bored. A bad time is when you're frustrated or angry or at a gathering.

Don't make jokes in the hope of retaliation. It's a great advice given by an experienced comedian.

Don't make jokes on your boss's behalf. This will not allow you to make a joke however it can keep you out of troubles in HR.

This is a joke every once in awhile and then it's gone, but you'll get plenty of chances to make use of this joke. The next time it is mentioned, you must increase it. The key is to select more numbers, however this isn't enough. It is necessary to increase it emotionally as well. It is important to behave as if you're disappointed.

"Hey Jason, how many students do you expect to receive for this month?"

"I'm in the 611s because I've had to give up several. It's just a matter of trying to work harder."

Goodwill showering, music, Fish and Keeping Out of trouble with HR

A humorous attitude can generate goodwill within the workplace. It can create a positive energy. Do not ruin that reputation in the process of creating negative energy. Avoid becoming the target of HR-related complaints. Keep your good impressions on the table.

Do not go to work without having shower. Take a shower every single all day. It is essential to take a shower every day. If, for whatever reason, you think that you could go to working without showering it is not the case. Showers are essential. You need deodorant. It is essential to have cologne. The smell must be pleasant. Everyone at work has an employee who showers only for interview. Don't be the guy. It's a problem that persists since there is no way to tell anyone that you're a stinky person. I'm requesting everyone who reads this book to shower every single day before going to work. It is my request to everyone who reads this book to inform whom you are sitting close to about what your current showering routine is. If they have more showers than you do, they should take additional showers. If you think you should cover up the number of showers you have taken in order to appear like that you are taking more showers than others you should take more showers. ALWAYS wear deodorant.

If you're permitted to play music while at work, don't listen to the same tune repeatedly. Don't do it. You're listening to someone other person's least favourite song. People hate it. They won't tell that to you. You shouldn't repeat the same song repeatedly.

Do not microwave fish!

Don't eat at your desk. The kitchen was designed to be for.

Check if any of your friends have an allergy to perfume or fragrances. It's more beneficial to smell great than bad, however when you're forced to choose either side, you'll fragrances are too appealing. But, too much of something good is just excessively positive thing. It is best to tone it down.

Finally, you should take your life not as than you take it. This is just an occupation. It's working. There isn't anyone, in a bed of death, has would ever wish they had laughed more. Therefore, make sure to make sure to laugh more. Have as much fun as you're able. I've spent too many years thinking I could have more money, acquaintances, or to be more. The mature person is able to turn off feelings of anger and depression. They don't want to. Be yourself, and just smile. You are 1,000 per cent more adored by family, coworkers and loved ones than you feel. For a conclusion, realize that you're 10 times more fun than you believe you're. Make a statement.

www.ingramcontent.com/pod-product-compliance
Lightning Source LLC
Chambersburg PA
CBHW071442080526
44587CB00014B/1961